Harriette Arnow

By WILTON ECKLEY

Drake University

 245

Twayne Publishers, Inc.   ::   New York

Copyright © 1974 by Twayne Publishers, Inc.

Library of Congress Cataloging in Publication Data

Eckley, Wilton.
  Harriette Arnow.

  (Twayne's United States authors series, TUSAS 245)
  Bibliography: p.
  1. Arnow, Harriette Louisa (Simpson) 1908-
PS3501.R64Z65   813'.5'2   73-18406
ISBN 0-8057-0023-4

Twayne's United States Authors Series

Sylvia E. Bowman, *Editor*
INDIANA UNIVERSITY

Harriette Arnow

HARRIETTE ARNOW

For Grace

Preface

WHEN Harriette Arnow was a young girl, her mother told her that, if she would learn to milk a new-cow that had been added to the farm, she could use any surplus milk money to buy a second-hand typewriter. She got the typewriter; and ever since, writing has been to her what "knitting and crocheting are to other women."[1] She has never been able to leave it entirely alone, nor has she ever wanted to. And the American literary chronical is the richer for it.

Mrs. Arnow could not, by most standards, be considered a prolific author — her bibliography consists of four novels, a few short stories, and two books of social history; but what she has produced has been uniformly good. The novels *Hunter's Horn* (1949) and *The Dollmaker* (1954) were among the best sellers of their time; and the two social histories, *Seedtime on the Cumberland* (1962) and *Flowering of the Cumberland* (1963), have been highly regarded by reviewers and those interested in the Cumberland area of Kentucky and Tennessee.

Along with *Mountain Path* (1936), her first novel, the books just mentioned represent a penetrating and comprehensive treatment of the life of the Southern mountaineer from his origins to his migration to the industrial cities of the North. The mountaineer, of course, has long been a subject for writers of fiction as far back as William Gilmore Simms. For the most part, however, he has been treated in a melodramatic and sentimental fashion. Mrs. Arnow makes a definite break with this tradition; and, combining an acute awareness of the realities of the mountaineer's life with a marked ability to tell a story, she has opened for her readers new aspects of a people and a section that, once important in the development of the United States, have again come into prominence — this time because of the heavy hand of poverty.

Mrs. Arnow's fourth novel, *The Weedkiller's Daughter* (1970), departs from the mountaineer motif and treats the problems of a fifteen-year-old girl in contemporary Detroit. Though not from the Kentucky hills, she represents many of the same characteristics as those of a number of Mrs. Arnow's earlier creations.

As a result of her realistic treatment of both rural and urban themes, Mrs. Arnow can claim a niche for herself in what is commonly called the "Southern literary renaissance." But, as is true of many other writers who have contributed to this renaissance, her contribution has gone almost unnoticed by scholars and critics. The tendency has been to focus on a fairly limited number of authors and credit them, as John Bradbury has pointed out, "with total responsibility for the South's modern contribution to American letters."[2] The authors so credited, moreover, are almost exclusively those "whose work fits the pattern prescribed by the South's New Critics."[3] And this credited group is led by William Faulkner.

Indeed, the problem for any contemporary Southern writer is exactly that postulated by Louis Rubin in a paper titled "The Difficulties of Being a Southern Writer Today: Or, Getting Out from Under William Faulkner."[4] Rubin is correct when he points out that it is impossible for today's Southern writer not to be influenced in some way by the Mississippian. One might add that it is highly improbable that any current Southern writer will be judged except in comparison or contrast with Faulkner — more precisely, the best Faulkner fiction. This tendency became quite apparent when in 1955 Mrs. Arnow's *The Dollmaker*, in a decision that shocked many reviewers, did not receive the National Book Award — but was named runnerup in favor of Faulkner's *The Fable*.

The purpose of this study is not to show that Harriette Arnow is as good as or better than William Faulkner — nor any other writer for that matter. Rather, in light of the dearth of critical study of her work, it attempts to discuss Mrs. Arnow as an author in her own right, making some assessment of her work both as art and as a vehicle toward a better understanding of the kind of people about whom she writes.

Chapter 1 presents a biographical sketch of Mrs. Arnow. While not a definitive biography, it covers her life from birth to the publication of *The Weedkiller's Daughter*, with considerable attention given to the early years because of their formative influence. In this chapter her works are mentioned incidentally as she was working on them and as they appeared in publication. The next six chapters discuss in some detail her novels, short stories, and social histories — Chapter 2 deals with *Mountain Path*; Chapter 3, with the short stories; Chapter 4, with *Hunter's Horn*; Chapter 5, with *The Dollmaker*; Chapter 6, with *Seedtime on the Cumberland* and *Flowering of the Cumberland*; and Chapter 7, with *The Weedkiller's Daughter*. Chapter 8 is a brief overview of Mrs. Arnow's literary achievement — an achievement that hopefully is not, at this point, finished.

WILTON ECKLEY

Drake University

Acknowledgments

I extend my deep appreciation to the following: Mrs. Harriette Arnow and her husband Harold for their unstinting willingness to provide me with biographical information and their warm hospitality; the Drake University Research Council for a monetary grant to help with research; Dr. Jacquiline Bull of the University of Kentucky Library for making Mrs. Arnow's papers available; the Macmillan Company for permission to quote; and my wife for editorial and critical advice.

Contents

Chronology

1908   Harriette Simpson born July 7, Wayne County, Kentucky.

1912   Family moves to Burnside, Kentucky.

1913   Family moves to the hill above Burnside.

1917   First effort at fiction: story about an old writing desk written for fourth-grade assignment.

1918   Family moves to Lee County in eastern Kentucky, where father works in oil fields. Year of great influenza epidemic. Simpson children kept home from school and taught by mother.

1919-   Attends St. Helen's Academy.
1920

1920-   Attends first year of high school at Stanton Academy.
1921

1921-   Attends Burnside High School. Graduated in 1924.
1924

1924-   Attends Berea College.
1926

1926-   Teaches in a Pulaski County, Kentucky, rural school for
1928   two years.

1928-   Attends University of Louisville. Takes Bachelor of Arts
1930   degree in 1930. Does practice teaching in spring, 1930.

1931-   Teaches and serves as principal of small high school in
1934   Pulaski County.

1934   Teaches in junior high school in Louisville. Spends summer at Conway Inn in Petosky, Michigan. Begins *Mountain Path*.

1934-   Goes to Cincinnati and works as a waitress. Reads widely in
1939   the novel. Publishes some stories in little magazines. *Mountain Path* published in August, 1936. Writes *Between the Flowers* (unpublished).

1939   Marries Harold Arnow, a newspaper reporter, in March.

They move to abandoned farm on Little Indian Creek of the Big South Fork of the Cumberland in Kentucky.

1941 Daughter Marcella born September 22.

1944 Story "The Hunter" published in *Atlantic*. Harold works for *Detroit Times*.

1945 Moves to wartime housing project in Detroit in January.

1946 Son Thomas born December 15.

1949 *Hunter's Horn* published.

1951 Moves to country out from Ann Arbor, Michigan.

1954 *The Dollmaker* published.

1960 *Seedtime on the Cumberland* published.

1963 *Flowering of the Cumberland* published.

1970 *The Weedkiller's Daughter* published.

CHAPTER 1

Poppies in the Cornfield:
Life and Times

THE American painter George C. Bingham painted in 1851, a picture of Daniel Boone leading a group of settlers into the promised land of Kentucky — for in Boone's day Kentucky was indeed the promised land. Nature, unsullied by human hands, lay before such settlers like a new Garden of Eden where man, having left behind on the other side of the mountain his corrupt institutions, could once again enjoy the beauty and sustenance of nature.

Perhaps old habits die hard, or perhaps the myth of the garden as seen by the artist was too far removed from the reality of man's everyday existence. Whatever the case, in something less than two hundred years man's exploitive tendencies drove him from the Garden, or the Garden from him; and what was once a New Eden has, ironically enough, become Appalachia, the very connotation of which is poverty in its most acute form. The land, true, is still rich in beauty and natural resources, but it is also "growing its third welfare generation" and has counties "where more than a third of the population is unemployed, where the government check — social security, welfare, aid to dependent children — is the prime source of income, and where some men are so far from their last job that it cannot properly be said that they have a trade at all."[1]

The problems of Appalachia — poverty, politics, poor education, unemployment — are too complex to be treated in this study, and they are mentioned at all only because they provide a kind of backdrop for the discussion of Southern-mountain fiction generally and of the life and art of Harriette Arnow specifically. Though Mrs. Arnow no longer lives near the Cumberland River, it and the land that it waters are still very much a part of her. "Two things," she said, in writing of her early years, "tied all time together; these had run through most of the stories to shape the lives of man, and so did they shape our lives and the lives of the people about us. These were the land and the Cumberland."[2] And, one might add, so did they shape the fiction and nonfiction that Mrs. Arnow has produced. Nature to her has never been an abstraction but something concrete and sustaining, something providing a solid foundation upon which to base a life-view. Thus, to appreciate fully her work, one must understand the deep feeling that she has for the Cumberland area and the people who live there, a feeling that started with her childhood and grew as she did.

I *Life on the Hill*

More likely than not, some of the early ancestors of Mrs. Arnow viewed Kentucky in much the same way as did those pioneers depicted by Bingham, for her people came over the mountains from Virginia and the Carolinas well before 1800 to find homes along the tributaries of Big Sinking Creek. With others like them, they "built a community, not only with substantial log houses for themselves, but by 1800 they were organizing and soon building a house for Big Sinking Baptist Church."[3] Strong people were these, both in their physical ability to live close to nature and in their religious fervor to know their God. The land promised much and it provided much. Though the people "could not compare in wealth with those who settled in the Middle Basin . . . neither did they know poverty. Hogs and cattle in the woods, plenty of horses, a few slaves, big log houses, an abundance of food, and good health."[4] And ever they had the land and a positive relationship to it.

Harriette Arnow herself was born in Wayne County, Kentucky, on July 7, 1908, the daughter of Elias Thomas Simpson and Mollie Jane (Denney) Simpson. At the time of Harriette's birth, Elias, like Mollie Jane before her marriage, was a rural schoolteacher. The pay, however, was quite low; and eventually, as his family increased, Elias was forced to seek more lucrative endeavors. When Harriette was four years old, he was offered a bookkeeping position in the little town of Burnside, Kentucky; and, despite an aversion for working with figures, he took it.

Burnside, at the time, was predominantly a lumbering town. Boasting a population of one thousand, five lumber mills, and a poultry processing plant, it carried the appellation of Head of Navigation of the Cumberland River; and it was also a major point on the Southern Railroad. Although opened to the world by steamboats and trains, and thus an exciting place for a child of Harriette's age, Burnside was, by almost any measure, a small town. "I remember," commented Mrs. Arnow, "the pats on the head, and wherever you went, candy was given to you. People knew you, called you by name, or if not by name, they knew you were one of the then three Simpson girls."[5]

Whatever its attractions for the children, Mollie Jane Simpson did not care for the life of the town; and, though not the head of her household, she guided its destinies when they did not guide themselves. Like many of her pioneer ancestors, she had an aversion to crowds and did not approve of her daughters' going among such, whether they be gathered for a religious revival, a circus or carnival, or a political speech; for she did not want her children's nerves or emotions aroused for either God or government. So, with her encouragement, Elias bought some thirty or forty acres of land high on a wooded hill above Burnside, and there he built a home for his family. The hill, facing west, provided striking sunsets on summer evenings; and, if one climbed a bit higher up the craggy bluff, he could have a sweeping view of the country for miles around — to the west, Burnside with its steamboats, trains, lumber mills, and neatly painted white houses; to the east the higher hills, streaked dark with coal, and that part of the Cumberland River where steamboats could not navigate. It was a good world for Mollie Jane, who, with six children and a husband to look after and always one or two dogs underfoot, knew much of reality, yet ever maintained a rather romantic view of life.

Mrs. Arnow described an incident illustrative of this characteristic of her mother:

I remember once we came trooping home from Sunday school, and found on the table some pies with a beautiful billowy golden meringue and a filling that looked dark around the edges. The eagerly awaited time for eating the pie came at last — but each of us took only one bite and then looked at our mother. The darkness of the filling had made us think that what we had was chocolate pie, and it was not chocolate pie, but pumpkin custard and terrible pumpkin custard at that, so thick with cloves and nutmeg and allspice that it burned our tongues. Our mother looked at us and wanted to know how we liked the chocolate pie, and when we tried to tell her that what we ate was pumpkin she would not listen but told us to use our imaginations, and could she help it if she forgot and put in all the spices twice and made it dark as chocolate. That was why she had made the meringue, not necessarily to make it taste better, but to help us imagine that it was chocolate.[6]

Just as they are to Mrs. Arnow today, flowers and gardening were always a part of Mollie Jane's life. The gardens around the house on the hill were not the usual pattern of neat rows of this and that but were more-or-less scattered plots with little design. Interspersed among the vegetables were bulbs, grape cuttings, peach seedlings, and flowers of all kinds; and it was a trial indeed for whoever agreed to plow the plots. The gardens would start out orderly enough in the spring, but soon would come the gifts of plants from friends and relatives. These, along with "the volunteers," would soon overflow the garden; for Mollie Jane never had the heart to pull a clump of fine daisies from the bean rows or to put a walnut seedling in its proper place or to clear the garden fence completely of the morning glories and trumpet vines and Virginia creepers or to dig up the wild white violets that were always in the way at the back of the barn. Young Harriette tried once to arrange an orderly garden of herbs — "something like the ones from which the ladies in *Silas Marner* doubtless gathered their lavender and thyme."[7] She bought seed and planted them in neat rows, but the garden did not thrive, proof "that in our lives the Irish and the French would triumph over the English and the Scot and the German and the Dutch. We in common with most hill people were a mixture of many nationalities, with all of the bloods mixed before the Revolution but somehow fighting still."[8]

Life on the hill for the Simpsons followed a kind of laissez-faire gentility, with the lives of the household guided mostly by the weather, their nerves, their distastes, and their desires:

Sometimes we all went to church on a Sunday; sometimes we stayed home. Sometimes we cooked dinner but no supper; sometimes we cooked both and sometimes neither, but set a great iron pot of green beans to boil in the yard and then put in potatoes and roasted ears of green corn in the ashes and boiled meat over the coals. Sometimes we would eat for weeks in the kitchen on blue or red checked table cloths, and then one day we would decide to be civilized and eat in the dining room with a white cloth on the table, use the little silver that we had, the good china and decorate with candles and proper flowers instead of the ironweed and the stick wood and the wild asters that were often scattered about the kitchen in vases or fruit jars. Sometimes we were roused at break of day; other mornings, when there was no school, not at all, but strolled downstairs and cooked what it pleased us to eat. We were supposed to eat eggs and a hot or cold cereal and some fruit, so some of us made omelets, and some waffles, but it made no difference to our mother. We had eaten the eggs. We started the preparation of a meal usually when somebody began to complain of being hungry and ate when the food was done.

We were a sore trial to the hired girls we now and then had and to the woman who did our washing. We did not wash on a certain day in the week, but usually when both the weather and our mother's nerves seemed suited to the work; and as it happened quite frequently that neither was not, the washerwoman was sent for only when everything on the place was dirty even to the linen towels and the good sheets and the sheets kept always carefully ironed and folded to be used when someone of us died.[9]

A significant influence on the children was Grandmother Denney, who liked order, pattern, and dignity, and who probably often wondered how she could have had a daughter like Mollie Jane. Grandmother Denney was indeed somewhat out of place in the world of the family, but then perhaps she "would have been out of place in any world. Some of her people had been on the wrong side in France, and had come away; then later they were on the wrong side in the Civil War. But whether a side won or lost it made no difference to Grandma."[10] She did her best to make ladies out of her granddaughters; and, while she lived, they wore fine tucked, lace-trimmed, stiffly starched underwear, kept their hair in curls, sat often with books on their heads to make them straight, and heard much talk of "good blood and bad blood and blood that was not blood at all."[11] Strongly religious, Grandmother Denney for more than thirty years after her husband's death wore black and grieved for him because he had died a member of no church and had surely gone to hell.

There were few diversions in Burnside that were considered acceptable for daughters, young or old. The one movie in town, the wandering circuses and carnivals, and local baseball games were forbidden. The once-a-year fair, a few picnics and birthday parties, and several church and school affairs provided the only social life for the children, leaving much time on their hands, even after the daily chores were finished. Making candy, baking cakes, sewing, riding the mules, walking in the woods, and visiting the river were common pastimes. Harriette early grew to love the outdoors — the rocks and trees of the hill and the immense sky overhead. A good world, it was one in which a child could wander alone with no fear of hurt; and Harriette did. She conjured up her own playmates and built play houses of stones. Along with her sisters, she made people in the sunsets, looking in the clouds and hunting faces and castles and worlds.

When she was about five years old, Harriette became aware of the stories that were being told all around her. Elias and Mollie Jane, like their people before them, were avid storytellers and singers; and they kept their children well entertained. Thus, Harriette early had an awareness of the other days and of her people — an awareness that was to pay rich dividends in later years. It was in these early years that the dim shapes of future interests began to take form. People then were not separated from their forebears as they are to-day. The past did not recede so rapidly into remoteness, and memories were fresher in the mind. Indeed, the older people lived on memories, but for Harriette they were not enough merely as memories. She had to put her imagination to work on them:

Sometimes I changed them to my liking; foggy times were good for this; and we had in fall and winter many still gray days when the sky was lower than our hill. Wraiths of fog wandered about all day long, and even when the rain stopped, the woods dripped still as from a heavy dew; and all sounds came clearly up from the hidden world below us like sound heard through water. At such times the cows did not stray far from the barn, and I was denied my favorite occupation — the hunting of our cows through the acres of the hill pasture above the house. Still, there was the walk home from school; first, down a lane that went past the graveyard where through the shifting fog any fresh grave glowed a bright red, for our land was a bright land of gray or white limestone and red earth, brighter yet when washed by the rain and contrasted with the dark green of cedar boughs that in fog or rain were darkened instead of brightened. There was a creek to cross, and then the road up the hill under the great cedars and over limestone ledges, some step-like, others higher, craggy and gray.

It was in the gray stillness with the smell of cedar, of wet earth, and the fainter smell of decaying limestone all about me, that I remade the memories as I wanted them to be. True there was confusion; the past, present, and the stories I was beginning to read were all mingled in my head.[12]

The stories told were not ones in the formal sense with a beginning and an end; they were more like reminiscences. Especially was Mollie Jane fond of recalling her childhood and her young womanhood when she had been a teacher in the hills. She loved horses and could remember clearly the characteristics of the horses she had ridden as a child and as a young woman. Nor was there a set story hour; storytelling, in a sense, went on all the time — stories by the minister, who, on his occasional visits, kept Harriette keenly interested with his accounts of missionary experiences in China; stories by Elias and his friends about the early days in the oil fields and about bringing logs down from the hills; stories of the old days by the washerwoman, whose mother had worked for Mollie Jane's grandmother.

Stories of witchcraft were common, but even more exciting were the ghost tales told by the best storyteller of all, the children's father. Thus, witches and the supernatural, to the children, seemed more-or-less a natural part of their lives and never too unreal. At Old Christmas, for instance, Harriette and her sisters would sneak out to the barn to see if the cattle were really kneeling at midnight, only to be disappointed to see them merely asleep as usual.

Many too were the stories handed down from both sides of the family about wars — the French and Indian War, the Revolutionary War, the War of 1812, and the Civil War. Those told by Mollie Jane more often than not portrayed war as seen through the eyes of women and were never so bloody or so terrifying as those told by Grandmother Simpson, who would frighten her grandchildren with vivid accounts of guerilla activities and atrocities during the Civil War — horses stolen, houses burned, and men killed in their sleep. South-central Kentucky was a divided area during the Civil War, some for the North, some for the South, and some neutral. Relative fighting against relative was not an unusual situation, nor was it among Harriette's people.

The stories told filled a unique place in the lives of the tellers and indeed of the hearers. They never seemed far away, not even the old ones that happened in Virginia and the Carolinas on the other side of the mountains. Harriette, in a sense, lived in two worlds on the hill — the world of civilization represented by Burnside and the world of nature and of the past represented by the hill itself. The world of the hill provided a continuity between the lives of the Simpson family and those of their people a hundred or more years before.

Even though Grandmother Denney disapproved of the daily paper, most magazines, and many books, reading was always an important part of the family's life and rivaled storytelling as a pastime. There was no library in Burnside other than the school library, and it was designed primarily for the reading habits of the high-school students. Most of the books, moreover, in the Simpson family were old — old histories, reference books, volumes of sermons, some poetry, McGuffey Readers, and Ray's Higher Arithmetics. The children read all that they could understand and looked fòrward with anticipation to each new school year and the new books to be read. A birthday might mean a new book, as would perhaps a trip to the county seat by one of the parents.

Christmas, however, brought the most books and probably the most excitement of the entire year. Following the Christmas Eve church pageant and the long walk across the little town and up the hill by lantern light, the family would enjoy hot homemade vegetable soup, slices of home-baked ham crusted with brown sugar and cloves, apples, tangerines, candy, and cake. When the smaller children were in bed, the older ones, Harriette included, would sneak into the cold north room and by candle light would play at being Santa Claus, carrying in the until-then hidden packages for all the family. The small square packages were the most tantalizing for Harriette, for there was an enchanting smell about them, "a smell of glue and new cloth such as comes in a small close country store when a bolt of new gingham is being unwrapped — and a tiny smell in whiffs and snatches like a new pencil tablet and a bottle of ink — a book or maybe two or three books together — what would they be — a wonder that would come in the waking moments of the rest of the night, for nothing on earth had quite the promise of a new book."[13]

Her sixth Christmas brought Harriette Johann Wyss's *Swiss Family Robinson* and Daniel Defoe's *Robinson Crusoe*. A little later came much of Dickens and John Bunyan's *Pilgrim's Progress* and at ten Alfred Lord Tennyson's *Idylls of the King*; and "the cloud people instead of merely battling the wind all day as was their usual custom were knights who at sunset lay dying, their blood and their golden armor and jewelled clothes scattered over half the western sky."[14] That same year brought "The Rime of the Ancient Mariner," and for Harriette the fog below her in the valleys became a sea as she read and reread the poem — soon committing half of it to memory.

Along with each story book given as a present were usually one or two educational books. These too were read from cover to cover — stories of the Bible, lives of great musicians and artists, myths of Greece and Rome, and local history books. But the story books appealed most to Harriette, giving her opportunity to let her imagination work. Usually, she had "to change them (the stories) in my head afterwards, give Maggie Tolliver a kinder brother, put a less fragile heart in the lily maid of Astolat and let no angel envy Annabelle Lee. Cedar tree and candle grease and glue, the smell lingers."[15]

II   *Pencils and Inkwells*

Early one September day in 1914, Harriette Simpson walked the path that led down low, limestone, craglike steps, then under the big cedars to the creek, and finally up the creek valley to the Burnside school, a red brick building housing all grades from one through twelve. As Kentucky hill schools went at that time, it was a good school. The first-grade teacher, a distant relative of Elias Simpson, was, as were indeed the other teachers in the school, a good storyteller. Imaginative Harriette could ask no more than that. She did well enough in her work, particularly enjoying reading and arithmetic — though penmanship and spelling posed some problems — and, the first four years of school were happy ones, filled with games, stories, art work, and most of all, new books to read:

> Although I suppose I wasn't aware of it, I was gradually drawing away from the world on the hill and I ceased to be the little sponge picking up more and more things. I began to read more. There were stories that I read over and over. I remember one of the Nuremburg Stove. This beautiful, beautiful porcelain stove. We used heating stoves — we didn't have central heating in our home and I remember looking at the iron stove and thinking how wonderful it would be to have a stove of porcelain. Another story that held my attention because I could more or less translate it into my own life was the "Valley of the Three Brothers Gluck," a wondrous valley where all things grew and prospered. I also enjoyed reading about the gods and goddesses of Greece and Rome and the gods of the North, such as Thor with his mighty hammer. And as these made use of many animals and objects, most of which were not alien to my world, once again I could enter into them.[16]

In the fourth grade, Harriette experienced one of the more significant triumphs marking her education. When the class was asked to write a story, Harriette wrote of the thing she had always wanted — a big writing desk full of cubby holes and drawers such as they used at the George P. Taylor plant where she sometimes took chickens to sell. She imagined such a desk and wrote of all the things that had happened to it throughout its life. The teacher, greatly impressed with the girl's efforts, read the story to the class, making the child very proud indeed.

Perhaps Harriette didn't realize it at the time, but childhood more-or-less ended with her completion of the fourth grade. Early in the summer Grandmother Denney died, giving the youngster her first intimate experience with death. Rural as Burnside was, birth and death were never very far from people's daily lives; for what often is taken care of in hospitals today was left to the home then. When someone died, neighbors would lay out the body since there was no undertaker in the community. Thus, though children were never supposed to know the facts of life, they could hardly avoid them; and Harriette grew more aware of the things that were happening to people around her: the deaths of two neighbor women who left children and of the circumstances at home — the ever-deepening poverty. There were now five children, and the debts were mounting.

She was also impressed by World War I, which America had just entered. She saw the war through the eyes of the women who stayed at home. Though she had no close relatives actually in the war, there were people who brought letters from men in it to be read to them by Mollie Jane or who dictated letters for her to write. The youngster was struck by the fact that there were in the world — her world — people who could neither read nor write. She was moved partly by pity for the people and partly by rebellion that there should be a world so made or set up that people could be that way. She could not conceive of a home where there was not a Mollie Jane or a Grandmother Denney to teach a child to read and write. But here were parents who had sons in France, yet had no idea what or where France was because they could not read a map. For them, war was truly loneliness and separation.

In the late summer of 1918, responding to the financial demands of the family, Elias Simpson journeyed alone to remote Lee County, where he took a job as a tool dresser in the oil fields. In the autumn of that same year, the great Asian influenza epidemic ravaged Burnside. Through the bare trees in front of the house the family could see almost daily new mounds of red clay in the graveyard, and Harriette again felt a sense of helplessness before an unseen power that her young mind could not understand. As the errand girl for the family, she continued to go down to the town; but Mollie Jane kept the rest of the children close to home. Her fear was such that she took all of her children out of school and taught them herself at home. By Christmas she had decided that she and the children would join Elias.

Mollie Jane was not happy in Lee County. Her health was not good, and she lived in constant dread of an accident involving Elias. Moreover, she loathed the raw ugliness of the oil fields. Harriette, however, found the sandstone ridges with straight up and down bluffs an exciting contrast to the gentle limestone contours around Burnside. The area was so rough that the oil rigs often had to be pulled by as many as eighteen yoke of oxen. Most fascinating of all were the sights, sounds, and smells of the actual drilling. Children were, of course, not permitted about a working oil rig; but, when taking her father's breakfast or dinner — drillers and tool dressers worked from twelve to twelve, Harriette watched as much as possible; and she learned the meaning of a few of the strange new words and phrases such as "bailer," "drill bit," and "bull wheels" that her father sometimes used at home.

Though only ten at the time, she was left with an indelible impression regarding the oil country and what was being done to it. In a letter to Harold Strauss, an editor for Covici-Friede, written late in 1939, she recalled this impression:

The country there was mostly high ridges and deep, narrow valleys and in it almost everywhere were signs of the things that had happened to it. Before the coming of the oil men, the lumbermen had come and gone and left it ugly with rotting limbs of trees and broken underbrush, and ruined saplings. They had not only taken, but they had destroyed just as the oil men destroyed everything they touched. Salt water was pumped out and left to flow at its will so that sometimes in the valleys one would come upon a great band of earth where the salt water had been allowed to run and everything was dead, even to the weeds and wild flowers. I suppose that I would have noticed and thought on things less had I not heard much talk of such matters at home. But I learned to hate something, almost like hating a man who came and ruined and stole and destroyed, and then went to another place to do the same thing. And at the same time, it seemed to me that there were places, the places where the oil money went that must be very good and fine and beautiful built as they were out of the destruction of the land, like the immense fortunes and the imposing businesses that have flowered out of the ugliness and the misery of the Harlan and Perry coal lands. It is as if the lands here and the people here have never existed for themselves, but as spawning grounds for the ones who are to go away and as the bedrock for the fortunes of shrewder, more money-minded people.[17]

In the early spring, influenza attacked the Simpson children, and a doctor was summoned from more than thirty miles away. Though one of the girls was critically ill, all recovered in time to enjoy the glories of spring in the new country. The valleys and ridges were like a vast garden of wild flowers — trillium, anemones, dog-tooth violets, rhododendron, and mountain laurel. Lover of growing things that she was, young Harriette was even more impressed with the land and its flowers and trees.

Since there was no school for miles, the children were again taught at home by Mollie Jane, who proved to be no permissive instructor: she worked her pupils hard and they learned well. The next year Harriette and her older sister were sent to a boarding school at St. Helens, Kentucky. Harriette was small for her eleven years, but with what excellent background she had received from Mollie Jane and the work of the teachers at St. Helens, she finished the work for the eighth grade and was ready for high school before she was twelve. Though her sister stayed on at St. Helens, Harriette, who did not care for the school despite her marked success there, was sent to Stanton Academy in Powell County, not far from where the family was living.

Stanton was a school endowed by the Presbyterian Church, and Harriette found it a pleasant place indeed. Religion was not particularly stressed, though there was a great deal of Bible reading in the off hours. Always good in memory work, Harriette memorized some fifty psalms she especially liked. Of the required courses — English, Latin, science, and mathematics — English, because of the writing it required, especially appealed to Harriette. At the request of her English teachers, she wrote a story and read it to the Literary Club of the Academy. It was a story about a boys' basketball game, and she was elated indeed for the opportunity to read it. Encouraged by a roommate who also had literary interests, she became more and more interested in writing. Though at the time they did not call it writing, the two girls tried composing poems; and they later exchanged many letters about their writing pursuits.

When the price of oil dropped sharply in 1920-21, the royalty checks Elias had been receiving from oil rights inherited from his father's land dwindled to almost nothing. Worse, the small oil company for which he worked stopped drilling operations. Out of work, he decided that the best thing for the family would be to move back to the house on the hill above Burnside. Harriette was able to stay at Stanton until the end of the term; but, even though they offered her a work scholarship for the following years, Elias and Mollie Jane decided it best for her to attend high school in Burnside. She was close to thirteen and able to do the work of an adult at home, and it was felt that she could be of much help to her somewhat ailing mother.

Feeling a bit rebellious because she was not to return to Stanton, Harriette moved in the spring to the house on the hill. The scenery was still as beautiful as ever, and she still enjoyed going out to hunt for the cows. Somehow, though, the glamor and the childhood wandering of the old days were gone. The cloud people were perhaps still there, but Harriette's mind, now preoccupied with household duties and with caring for the baby just born to Mollie Jane, did not see them. Even the start of school that fall failed to brighten her outlook significantly. Perhaps for the first time in her life she felt genuinely unhappy, but part of her problem was probably the usual unhappiness of adolescence. She had, however, been promoted two years, so that the children she had known in the first four grades in Burnside were now two years behind her. Once again she was with strangers. She never particularly minded strangers, but, because of her age and size, it seemed to her that she was regarded as a bit of a curiosity.

Burnside High School, in contrast to Stanton Academy, was a disappointment to Harriette. It offered only two years of Latin; and, since she had already had one, she had only one more to take. The teaching, too, suffered somewhat when compared with that of Stanton. One bright aspect of the curriculum, however, was her agriculture class. Under the Smith-Hughes Act, Burnside was able to hire an excellent teacher of agriculture; and, though not particularly interested in farming, Harriette's passion for growing things, for watching seeds sprout, for finding a strange flower, and for wondering how plants fed themselves or how they actually got nourishment from the sand and sun made this class a most interesting one — one that opened wider worlds for her and increased her curiosity. History, too, provided stimulation for Harriette: "Once again we began with the ancient world and we gradually worked our way through until we had English History in the Junior year, and then we studied American History. By the time we finished, if we had any comprehension at all, I think we had a much better idea of the origins of our laws and the Constitution than a child of today gets who studies no history except that of the United States. We knew that our government had not sprung fully grown from the soil of Colonial America."[18]

Perhaps the happiest moments for Harriette during the years at Burnside High came from extracurricular activities. The literary and debating societies met once a month, and she was active in these. More often than not, such meetings ended in what the students referred to as "games" but what would more accurately be labeled "dancing." In a community that frowned on even "Skip to My Loo," these games were indeed daring adventures to the young people. Once they tried the Virginia Reel, really bringing down the wrath of many of their parents, who considered that as out and out dancing. The young people never went any farther than folk dancing and, of course, did not try couples because the whole town would have been shocked.

Probably the real point of dissention and what made Harriette so lonely at home involved her writing. She had little thought of making money from writing or even of publishing anything, yet the compulsion to write was constantly there; but it was frowned upon by her parents as a waste of time and energy, even though they, like the rest of the town, were proud of the one writer Burnside had produced. This was Edith Fitzgerald, a writer of short stories, some of which appeared in the *Saturday Evening Post*. Miss Fitzgerald, who no longer lived in the town but whose family did, may not have been an idol of Harriette's, but she was an object of the girl's admiration. In addition to writing for the *Post*, Miss Fitzgerald also did some script writing for Hollywood; but, since movies were frowned upon by Burnside elders, Harriette had no opportunity to see any of her products. Through her reading, however, she knew about Hollywood. That kind of writing didn't interest her, yet she felt that, if Edith Fitzgerald could do it, she might be able to do it too.

At this time a very wonderful thing so far as Harriette was concerned happened. She typed out a story, a fairy tale about the flowers in the nearby valley, and sent it to *Child Life*. Knowing nothing about submitting stories, she had single spaced it on small-sized stationery. Shortly in the mail came a large envelope from *Child Life* containing her story, neatly typed, double spaced on regular-sized typing paper, and a letter stating that the editors had torn the story and felt that they should retype it. ". . . I have often wondered," she reminisced, "if someone realized this was practically a child — I was around 14 or 15 — a very ignorant person and they wanted to give her a very gentle lesson in how a story should be submitted. From that day on I began to think that editors or typists or whoever had done it were very nice people. Of course in later years it was sometimes necessary to change my mind."[19]

During her high-school years, though she never submitted another story to a publisher, and despite the absence of any encouragement, Harriette worked hard on her writing. It seemed as if she would never again enjoy life as she did in the earlier years on the hill. The sadness, the dreariness, and the worry about life in general rested heavily on the mind of the young girl. One of the most depressing things was the question of her future. While women in the 1920's were reaching out more than ever before for places in the various professions and in the business world, Harriette's parents were quite adamant about their decision that their daughters would be teachers. After all, hadn't both Elias and Mollie Jane been teachers? What better way of earning a living until marriage could there be for a girl? One sister was already attending normal school, and the decision was made that Harriette, too, should follow this route. After two years in college, she would be, as her mother had been, ready to teach at eighteen. So, with some lack of enthusiasm, Harriette chose Berea College.

III *Berea*

Life at home for the Simpson children was never in any real sense regimented. Though Elias and Mollie Jane, and certainly Grandmother Denney, were extremely pious and religious people and might in some manner be strict about such things as the use of slang or the kinds of social activities in which their children participated, they never imposed any truly hard and fast rules. They never lectured their offspring but merely expected them to do what was right, and usually the children did. At Berea, however, Harriette found life quite different from what she was used to. She had chosen Berea because it seemed to offer the widest opportunity for taking courses in areas that interested her and did not require a preponderance of pedagogical studies. But, failing to read the college catalogue carefully, she was quite unprepared for the kind of life that Berea offered and demanded of its students — a Christian life, complete with labor, dress, and social regulations. She hardly needed a Christian education because she had been reared in the church and on the King James version of the Bible. But, need it or not, Harriette was to get it during her stay at Berea.

Berea operated under a rather stringent set of rules. Clothing restrictions, for example, were somewhat severe; and the many pairs of silk hose that Harriette received as graduation presents had to be left in a trunk at home. Girls were never permitted to roll their stockings or to show any bare skin except on the arm and a small area of the neck. Also, it was strictly forbidden to go from gymnasium class across the campus without changing clothes because the required uniform of black bloomers was suggestive. "Suggestive" was a popular word at Berea, so much so that it was not used merely as an adjective but was made into a proper noun. Yet on Mountain Day, each girl was supposed to blossom fourth in her middie blouse and her black bloomers with a date. Harriette, though shy, had her share of dates; but it had been drilled into her so long and so hard that it was a sin to go around in black bloomers that she couldn't help but feel self-conscious. With all of these restrictions to be concerned about, Harriette looked forward with much anticipation to the Sunday afternoon hikes which were permitted women if they went in the sole company of other proper women.

Students at Berea were required to work, or more specifically, to labor. It was the word "labor" that bothered Harriette. At home she had always worked, and her father had never been ashamed to go out and work with his hands to help support his family. She was accustomed to work, but she had never heard it called "labor" as it was at Berea. Labor at Berea was enforced, and such enforcement for Harriette was necessary because she would rather have been reading, or folk dancing, or doing a great many other things. The ten cents an hour that students were paid was, of course, necessary for her also. In addition to washing dishes, she worked two hours a day at Fireside, a place where thread was woven into cloth for towels, tablecloths, and various other products to be sold to tourists. It was at Fireside one day that Harriette had perhaps one of her most unpleasant moments while at Berea:

And I suppose it was because I was young with a rather stupid look, I don't know why, but this woman with an accent very different from the ones I knew, more like those of our teachers at Berea, was watching the work. She came around and watched me for a while and then she said, "Can either of your parents read or write?" My reaction was violent. I didn't move. I just tried to imagine my parents, my home, my grandparents, my great-grandparents, both great-grandfathers — there were stories of their books and their books still around — without books and newspapers like those poor, pitiful people unable to read who would come to get my mother to write letters — but I only had one wish: to get that woman away from me and I felt that if I said, "Of course, they can read," she might ask more questions, so I said, "No, neither can read or write." She was satisfied. She had guessed correctly. She walked on and I made up my mind then that no matter where I went or what I did I would never, never be a tourist and ask people direct, personal questions.[20]

While many aspects of Berea were a trial to Harriette, the academic work was a pleasure to her inquiring mind; and she worked hard at geology, botany, and English literature. She continued too with her writing, but there was never a word of praise for any of it. Her botany teacher offered to get her a scholarship to pursue futher study in botany or, failing that, to loan her the money himself. But once again family obligations intervened, forcing her to leave Berea and take a teaching position. Her older sister had been teaching and now wanted to return to college; therefore, at her parents' insistence, Harriette, not quite eighteen, returned home to begin a new career.

IV   *A Touch of Reality*

At the time Harriette left Berea, teaching positions were difficult to find, particularly for a young girl with no experience. With the help of her father, however, Harriette obtained one in her home county in a remote school in a valley up the Cumberland River from Burnside. No more than fifteen miles across country from Somerset, the county seat, which had one of the best school systems in the state, this school was in an area where such luxuries as cars and radios were essentially unknown; and it was with a great deal of self-pity and trepidation that Harriette, turned eighteen just two days before, alighted from the train that had carried her to within eight miles of the valley where the school was located. She was met by a trustee of the school district, who put her on a mule and led her along winding ridges to his home, a log structure like all the others of the community. The beauty of the country made no small impression on Harriette, and it helped to mitigate her self-pity at being forced to leave the amenities of a more civilized world.

The young neophyte teacher was soon ensconced in her boarding place, a rather large log house not far from the school and near the river. For the first time in her life, Harriette enjoyed the luxury of a room all to herself — a snug upstairs room with its own small fireplace. The food in the home, mostly home grown and quite abundant, included everything from canned wild strawberries to the standard fare of fried chicken and pork. The open friendliness of the people and their hospitality caused her to reevaluate her original, negative reactions at being exiled to a backwoods community. "I was able to join in the life of the people. They invited me. Often we walked or rode muleback together to church. I remember molasses stiroffs and music parties and a rousing charivari — mostly shotgun blasts — for a wedding. The mail came three times weekly by muleback to the village. There were no postboxes, so we would go around to the post office to get the mail. Other times I went with the landlady across the Cumberland to another store."[21] Though she may not have realized it at the time, Harriette was in the midst of the kinds of experiences she was to write into the novel *Mountain Path* not too many years hence.

The school boasted about fourteen children; and the attendance of these was quite sporadic, especially in the winter when the three-or-four-mile journey that some of them had to make by foot became difficult. Like most of the rural schools of that day, this one was sparsely equipped. On opening day Harriette was astonished and chagrined when she walked into the school, which could not be locked because the lock had been shot off, and found nothing inside but a few wooden benches, a table, a stove, and a lot of dirt. With a water bucket and broom that she had with her, she cleaned the place, arranged the books on the table, and opened the school.

The children were intelligent enough but had practically no intellectual or cultural background. The community had no daily newspaper and no books, save a few Bibles. Even Sears Roebuck catalogues were a rarity. Moreover, no one in the area had even gone to high school because there was none to go to. The only possibility would have been boarding school, an alternative that was, of course, financially impossible. Harriette for the first time became acutely aware of poverty. Her own family, though far from affluent, had always taken physicians, dentists, and the like for granted; but in this community, such things were not even luxuries — they were nonexistent. Birth, illness, and death all took place in the home and were attended to by neighbors. There was no shortage of food, but money was scarce. Unlike the people around Burnside, these people had no outlet for their extra butter, eggs, or milk. The closest market was miles away and over very difficult terrain. Some of the men in order to get cash would go to work in the winter to mines farther east, returning in the spring to put in their crops.

Harriette could not long maintain the self-pity she had felt upon her arrival in the community, for the hardships of her students and the need of almost all the people there touched her deeply. The land, with the exception of a few pieces located in the valley, was not fit for farming; and Harriette wondered what would become of the children after they left school. She knew that they would have to leave because there was indeed little for them in the area. Lumbering had declined, and mining during the 1920's did not offer the possibilities that it had during the earlier years. Harriette wanted to write of these things about which she wondered; and, while taking a correspondence course in the short story at the University of Kentucky, she worked hard at describing the scenes around her, turning them into stories. Ironically enough, however, her grades were not good — mostly "C's" and "D's" — but she received no critical comment on any of her efforts. In connection with the course, she did do considerable reading of masters of the short story, reading which she enjoyed greatly and which was providing a foundation for her own later writing.

V   *To the City*

With the end of the school year, Harriette returned home, hoping to find time to continue writing. The demands of her family, however, were so great that she took another teaching position — this time as principal of a two-year elementary school within four miles of her home. This position was much more demanding and much less rewarding than the previous one; and Harriette, at the end of the year, went to Louisville with the determination to do no more teaching until she had at least completed a bachelor's degree.

Louisville offered a quite different life from what she had been used to: a large public library, vaudeville, good movies, an art museum, and the University of Louisville. She enrolled at the university, working at odd jobs to pay her tuition, room, and board. During her second year, she borrowed a few hundred dollars from the Kentucky Federation of Women's Clubs that enabled her to live at the Young Women's Christian Association and to devote full time to her studies. Despite the death of her father, she was able to continue until she took her degree in 1930.

During the period in Louisville, Harriette grew considerably, intellectually and culturally; and, even more important, she became more-or-less firmly wedded to the idea of writing. Coming into contact for the first time, as it were, with a wide array of people, some of whom were also interested in writing, Harriette soon forgot the loneliness of trying to write among people who thought it queer or funny. She wrote whenever she could find the time, and she belonged to Chi Delta Phi, a small literary group, which met once a week for lunch to listen to the results of latest efforts of its members. These years in Louisville provided Harriette with experiences and opportunities needed to bring her imagination to a new level of sharpness and sophistication from that which was nurtured by the trees, rocks, and sky of the hill.

But Harriette knew too that she had to earn a living and, moreover, that she could not earn it through writing. To complicate matters, there was need for money at home; therefore, Harriette returned once more to teaching — this time in the new rural high school in Pulaski County, an entirely different community from the one where she had done her first teaching. Somerset, the county seat, was not far; and there were books and magazines in the homes. Like many communities in the Kentucky hills, this one was prosperous; and a great many of its students went on to high school. Although a pleasant place to teach, Harriette's desire was still to live in a city; so when, about the middle of the second year, an opening arose in a Louisville junior high school, she took the position.

Living in Louisville again was good enough, but some of the harsher realities of teaching confronted Harriette, whose challenge it was to teach social studies to six groups of adolescents divided according to their intelligence quotients. Four of her groups contained pupils with the lowest scores in the school, as well as the worst discipline problems; indeed, some could not even read. Physically, the job proved too much for Harriette; at the end of four months, she was in the hospital with low blood pressure and a form of anemia. The following summer found her convalescent but broke — the demands of her family and her illness having left little from the hundred dollars she had received monthly as a teacher. She went to a resort in Northern Michigan where she had worked as a waitress during one vacation from college. This time, however, she went there not only to work but also to write. It was, in a sense, a kind of declaration of independence for her; for she was leaving teaching for good. The children at home were growing up, thus easing the financial pressures; and Harriette could now move out on her own. At the resort, she began to work on what was to become her first novel — *Mountain Path*.

In midautumn, she decided to go to Cincinnati to work as a waitress and to devote as much time as possible to writing. With its usual propriety, her family objected to such a plan, warning her that she was throwing away her education and, indeed, perhaps her whole life; in fact, her doing so was a scandal. But, scandal or no, Harriette was determined, and to Cincinnati she went. The Depression hung heavy over the city, but she was able to find a job in one of the better restaurants. The work was not hard nor the hours long, and Harriette had considerable time in which to continue her writing. But more than that, she was to come into contact with the vital life of the city again.

Cincinnati in the 1930's was quite an interesting place — a city where the old German culture mingled with the beginnings of the invasions from the South. Then too, there were the old, old families who had migrated westward from the colonies during the eighteenth century. German bands, strolling musicians, the call of newspaper boys — all filled the streets with sounds. The largest town she had ever known, Cincinnati was probably for Harriette what London was for Boswell. She made the acquaintances of other writers and editors who gave encouragement; and, when one suggested that she try writing for the "pulp" magazines, Harriette dutifully bought a stack of them to see just what the stories they contained were like. When she could not even finish the first one, she threw the rest in the trash and discarded the idea of trying to duplicate that kind of writing.

During her stay in Cincinnati, Harriette also became more cogently aware of what was going on in the world. Close to the restaurant where she worked was a newsstand where the *New Masses* and the *Daily Worker* were on sale; and, having heard so much about the proletariat, Harriette decided to learn what she could about them through reading in magazines and books. What she found, however, disappointed her. Or perhaps it would be better to say what she did not find: she did not find people treated as individuals, only as faceless masses. Her own background in the hills had taught her that even illiterate, humble people could carry on an organized and meaningful life and that such people were not without insight and emotion.

Mapping out a study of the novel for herself, Harriette began reading widely in English, Russian, and French literature. She was particularly impressed with Wladyslaw Reymont's *The Peasants* and Emile Zola's *Germinal.* In her earlier years at home she had become acutely aware of the attempts to unionize the mine in counties to the east of Burnside; and, perhaps inspired by Zola, she wished to go to Harlan, Kentucky, and "do a good novel of the mines. Once again it may be the kind of thing that would have to be done by a man — who would have access to the actual mine and know the miners. Still, I don't know. It would have been fun to have given it a try."[22]

VI *Breaking into Print*

Many of the things that Harriette read during her stay in Cincinnati began to merge with the things she was experiencing and had experienced; but the predominant influence, the one that "more-or-less colored all the rest of my life,"[23] was her early life on the hill; and more than ever she was drawn to write of the hills. She succeeded in publishing some short stories, one in the old *Southern Review,* then edited by Robert Penn Warren. She also continued with the writing she had begun in Northern Michigan, more a series of character sketches set in the hills than a novel. She sent it to Macmillan, where an editor, after keeping it for four months, rejected it with a very encouraging letter that left Harriette not too disappointed.

In the meantime she had a short story published in *New Talent,* a little magazine, which was seen by Harold Strauss, an editor for Covici Friede. He wrote asking if she had anything else she was working on, and she eagerly sent off the manuscript of sketches then titled *Path.* Strauss was impressed with her work, complimenting her on the delicacy and beauty of her style and referring to the book as "one of those rare volumes which, as the Macmillan people say, belong in no regular class but have such extraordinary quality of their own as to be completely self-justifying."[24] Strauss, however, had some reservations about *Path.* He felt that, as a series of sketches, it would meet with considerable opposition from the editors and, indeed, from a reading public, which had long since grown accustomed to novels, not sketchbooks. He thus urged Harriette to use what she had as the "basis for a dramatic novel, or at least one in which a major line of narrative continuity shall be inserted."[25]

After some exchanges of correspondence regarding changes and additions to *Path,* he wrote, "you must rewrite *Path,* and rewrite it immediately and devote a maximum amount of your energy to it. I can see that your ability as a writer has reached the point of fruition, or at least a point of first fruition; to delay any longer would be to malinger. Both what you have done already and your letters show me that I can leave the final determination of the problems which *Path* has evoked to you. My duty seems only to spur you on."[26] Following Strauss's advice, Harriette did rewrite *Path;* and, with its title changed to *Mountain Path,* it was published by Covici Friede in 1936.

Mountain Path might be termed autobiographical in the sense that Harriette drew on her school-teaching experience in the hills as a basis for the novel though the plot itself is purely fictitious. It is the story of Louisa Sheridan, who takes a teaching position in a remote Kentucky district and becomes involved in the problems of the family with whom she boards. Feuding, moonshining, and romance spice the plot; but close attention to character and scene takes the story beyond sheer melodrama, making it one of the better portrayals of Kentucky hill life of its time.

The novel was quite well received by the reviewers but, unfortunately, not by Harriette's family. It didn't approve of the book and felt she should have written about nicer people. One headline in particular, which appeared in a Cincinnati newspaper, upset the family: "Waitress Writes Book." Having worked as a waitress was bad enough, but writing a book on top of it was almost too much. Harriette's hopes that some good reviews of the book might help to heal the breach with her family were never realized. Its members were ashamed of the book and felt rather strongly about it, "afraid someone would think I had fallen in love with a moonshiner, and so on and so forth."[27]

Shortly after the publication of *Mountain Path,* Harriette began another novel — one again set in the mountains of Kentucky and entitled *Between the Flowers.* When it was finished, she sent it to Covici Friede, where Harold Strauss was still an editor. This novel, however, was never to be published, perhaps because it was a premature attempt at a second novel or perhaps because Harriette and Strauss were never able to agree on the development of its main characters. Strauss did spend a good bit of effort on the book, as did Harriette; and many letters were exchanged between the two.

Strauss encouraged her to write with more Realism and less melodrama; but, though she tried, she was never able to satisfy the editor. She read Realists like James Farrell, Vardis Fisher, and Meyer Levin in an effort to grasp what Strauss wanted. She readily agreed that they were good and that they made money, but she could not see herself following in their footsteps:

I suppose that I am mid-Victorian or possibly worse and I dislike such things, not because they might shock me or such, but because, though they may be realism, they are not necessarily true. If you graph the cosine using only two sets of variables, you would have a straight line or if you took only certain selected values you would get a set of broken lines, but if you took enough values as they came, working each as you worked the other and rejected no equation but plotted them all, then and then only would you get an indication of the curve of the cosine. Those men have taken certain selected points, rejected everything else and in some cases have drawn their lines distorting the whole picture of their original equation of man and some have not even bothered to draw a line but taken a few selected points flung them out with no connecting lines and called it realism.[28]

Following her failure with *Between the Flowers,* Harriette did some writing for the Federal Writers Project. Mostly booklets about early Cincinnati, the writing was not particularly stimulating for her; but she did become aware of the wealth of historical and social material available in manuscript form — an awareness that eventually enabled her to write *Seed Time on the Cumberland* and *The Flowering of the Cumberland.*

VII *Marriage*

Early in 1938, Harriette met Harold Arnow, a newspaper man from Chicago who was in Cincinnati looking for a job, and who had just returned from three years in Alaska where he had been gathering material that he intended to publish in a book. With their common interest in writing, the two spent much time together during the ensuing year. The relationship soon became one of love, and on a cold Depression day in March, 1939, they were married in a simple service in Kentucky.

Harold wanted a place where he could have the peace and quiet necessary to turn his Alaska material into book form; and, of course, Harriette also wanted to continue writing. So, with much enthusiasm and little forethought, the couple bought a strikingly beautiful piece of land at a very low price on Little Indian Creek of the Big South Fork of the Cumberland. The old log house on the land needed much repair, but in their desire to escape to the woods the couple saw this need as no obstacle and gaily named the place "Submarginal Manor" and moved in. But, while the simple life held much promise in theory, it presented many difficulties in actuality. For one thing, Harold fell in love with animals; and, instead of the couple of milk cows that had been envisioned, Submarginal Manor soon boasted a host of cattle, sheep, and pigs — and the work that went with providing for these creatures. Because of the lack of a market, there was little financial reward for this work. Moreover, the house had none of the conveniences typical of a town dwelling. All the water came from a spring, and heat was provided by coal that could be had on the place for the digging. Cheap though it was, this kind of heating brought much dirt. "I had never lived in a house that used coal," Mrs. Arnow recalled, "because even the very poor hill people refused coal. But Harold was no axe man so we used it."[29]

Tragedy struck the Arnows in December, 1939, when their first child was stillborn. Following her recovery, Harriette, perhaps in an effort to forget what had happened but also to help with the family finances, returned to teaching — this time in another one-room school. The responsibilities of teaching, along with the strenuous and somewhat precarious life at Submarginal Manor, left little opportunity for her writing; but Harriette was able to begin another novel — one that ten years later became *Hunter's Horn*. With Harold's encouragement and help, she developed a fragment of it into the short story "The Hunters" that was published by the *Atlantic Monthly*. In addition, she wrote a couple of articles for the *Writer's Digest*.

A daughter, Marcella, was born to the Arnows in September, 1941; and, with her arrival, both Harriette and Harold began to realize that they were really ill equipped to care for children in their beautiful but remote hill home. Any illness was a terror because of the distance to the nearest doctor and because of the poor condition of the roads, especially in bad weather when it might well be impossible to get out at all. With some sadness, Harold early in 1944 went to Detroit, where he secured a reporter's job with the *Detroit Times*. Harriette stayed behind for a time to sell the cattle and other animals and then followed.

World War II was still on, and Detroit, a city teeming with defense workers, faced a severe housing shortage. Harold managed to find an apartment in a temporary housing development, and the family moved into a place that was a striking contrast to anything that Harriette had ever been used to. The people, of all religious and economic backgrounds and from various sections of the country, were poured into the boiling cauldron of life in a wartime city; and this situation provided her a rich background against which she would exert her imagination in the writing of *The Dollmaker:*

Here, the same learning begun during my first year of teaching was intensified; that is the realization that most of us, regardless of our backgrounds, have a common bond. We are human beings. Most women I met were like myself in that they, too, were wives with children, all of us because of the war, uprooted to follow our husbands to Detroit. During my second spring there, I was out much with the baby in a little red wagon; sometimes going for groceries, but often just to air the baby; big enough to sit alone, she [Marcella] preferred the wagon to her carriage. I met other women doing the same thing; many wanted to stop and talk; and so we did, of those things we had in common: the war, our children in school, our babies, and often of flowers; many of us were trying to grow flowers in the small plots of earth around our little — units — we called our dwelling places. We grew to know each other better than those who study "the migrant" by statistics built on direct questioning can ever know. Such casual meetings with people is something else one misses in the country.[30]

Writing and housewifery did not make an easy combination, and Harriette was hardpressed to find time for her writing. Yet it was here in the crowd — by getting up at four o'clock in the morning to work for a few hours before her family awoke — that she finished *Hunter's Horn* and began *The Dollmaker*. And it was here, too, that son Thomas was born on December 15, 1946.

VIII   *Literary Fruition*

Hunter's Horn was published by Macmillan Company in 1949. Set in the hills of Kentucky, it is the story of a man's obsession to hunt down and kill King Devil, a fox who has an uncanny ability to evade every foxhound in the area and even to lead some of them to their destruction. As the reader follows Nunn Ballew's efforts to get King Devil, he becomes aware of the richness of the material from which the author has woven the fabric of her story. Far from being

just another hillbilly novel, *Hunter's Horn* is a realistic treatment of
life in the Kentucky hills that is presented with a thorough understanding of the people and their ways. The novel was a much
greater success than was *Mountain Path*; indeed, it should have
been, for it is a much better novel. As her second novel, it was a long
time coming, but for her the results were worth the waiting.

Not long after the publication of *Hunter's Horn,* Harold Arnow
decided the family would enjoy the country more than the city. Buying some acreage near Ann Arbor, they built a house; and, until recent years when housing developments sprang up around them, they
enjoyed the remoteness of country living. Yet Mrs. Arnow, though
she enjoys walking through their woods, growing flowers, and
feeding birds has never been overly enthusiastic about it:

And it's a life, when you look at it, that doesn't make too much sense because
my husband drives daily about one hundred miles back and forth to Detroit
to his work and while the children were home and in school it meant a second
car and I drove them back and forth to school just as I suppose hundred of
thousands of other mothers so situated do. It didn't leave too much time for
writing. My problems I suppose are like the problems of a great many other
women who hope to carry on after marriage and discover they cannot do as
they did before. I especially enjoyed reviewing books. There is something
about reviewing a soon-to-be-published book, then comparing your opinion
with that of other published reviews, and following the career of the book, I
find interesting, even exciting at times. But if I wanted to do any work of my
own at all in this rather mixed up life, I could not review books so that was
dropped. I had never had time to try short stories again because a short story,
at least for me, requires some time and concentrated effort. You can't just
stop it and start again.[31]

But, despite these handicaps, she did complete *The Dollmaker*.
For this novel, published by Macmillan in 1954, Mrs. Arnow turned
to wartime Detroit for a setting. The story is of a Kentucky hill
woman who moves to Detroit with her family when her husband gets
a job in a defense plant. Gertie Nevels is a strong woman, but she
finds city life difficult and at times incomprehensible. She can only
watch as it impinges upon her and upon her family, and threatens to
destroy the values that in the Kentucky hills were basic ones. Bringing out with clarity the conflicts of different value systems as they
meet in a wartime housing project and presenting a gallery of varied
characters, all well-drawn, *The Dollmaker* is a powerful, moving

novel that became a best seller and that ranked second to Faulkner's *The Fable* for the National Book Award in 1955.

Though caring for a husband and rearing a family might not have left much time for writing fiction, Mrs. Arnow did find the time to do the research for and to write two books of social history about the Cumberland area — *Seed Time on the Cumberland* (1960) and *The Flowering of the Cumberland* (1963), both published by Macmillan. Based on a plethora of documents and letters, these books present the Cumberland from prehistoric through pioneer times; and they clearly show that Mrs. Arnow's talents go beyond fiction writing.

Several years were to pass before Mrs. Arnow was to turn again to writing. Moving again to fiction, she wrote a novel titled *The Weedkiller's Daughter,* published by Knopf in 1970. Set in Detroit, this novel does not deal with Kentucky hill people but with a bright fifteen-year-old girl who rebels against what she sees as the phoniness and hypocrisy of the contemporary adult world; and she displays in the process many of the same characteristics that Louisa Sheridan, Suse Ballew, and Gertie Nevels did in earlier novels.

Harriette Arnow has never lost either her love for her homeland or her interest in people and in writing. She has successfully combined a career in writing with that of wife and mother, and both have no doubt been the better for it. What she will write in the future remains to be seen, but what she has written has distinction. She does not really consider herself a novelist or a historian, but a mere storyteller. The world, however, needs storytellers, if for no other reason than to keep its perspective. As Mrs. Arnow so well put it, "I think all of us need a few poppies in our cornfield to relieve the tedium of hoeing corn."[32]

CHAPTER 2

The Hills Beyond

IN the Introduction of the paperback edition of *Mountain Path,* Mrs. Arnow comments that it "was not an apology for a moonshining family; it tried to be only a story." Anyone reading the novel will have no difficulty in accepting this assertion; for, though it is the least of Mrs. Arnow's four novels, *Mountain Path* does not fall into the sentimental tradition of most mountain fiction up to that time. A Realist, Mrs. Arnow was recording a way of life that by now has largely passed, but that in the 1920's and 1930's was still prevalent in the remote valleys and hollows of the Cumberland area. It was a way of life that she, as a teacher in a one-room school more-or-less lost in the hills of Kentucky, came to know intimately.

Mountain Path is the story of an outsider who comes into the mountains with little or no background for understanding the people and their ways. The outsider in this case is Louisa Sheridan, a beginning school teacher from Lexington who accepts a position in remote Cal Valley (Kentucky) and steps into an intrigue of feuding and moonshining. The Cals (Calhouns), with whom she boards, are very much involved in the situation and try to keep Louisa from learning what is going on. Piece by piece, however, she puts together the details of the trouble and the Cals' part in it. In the process, she falls in love with Chris Bledsoe, a member of the Cal clan who, having killed a sheriff's deputy in revenge for his younger brother's murder, is a fugitive from the law. In the end, Chris is killed; and an emotionally mature Louisa prepares to return to Lexington.

Thus, on the surface, *Mountain Path* is just another melodramatic story of the mountains that is complete with suspense, violence, and romance. And the plot, in this sense, is interesting enough; but it is not really the crux of the novel. On the contrary, the plot exists primarily to provide continuity for the presentation of a gallery of mountain people and, indeed, of a whole way of life.

I *A Kind of Lost Like Place*

The opening scene of *Mountain Path* is very much like a painting — a dusty courthouse square of a small Kentucky hill town on a hot summer day. But it is not a still life; for, inconspicuous as it may be, there is movement in this picture. A tall hill man, with an unconscious grace, methodically cuts neat cubes from a muskmelon and conveys them on the knife blade to his mouth. This particular scene is important as more than just an opening for a story. Every story, to be sure, needs a setting, a playing field, as it were, for the characters who stream from the author's imagination. In this novel, however, setting and theme are inseparable.

Reflected in the courthouse-square tableau is the whole world of the mountains into which Louisa Sheridan is about to move. Fresh from the university at Lexington, she is a city girl whose urban sophistication is turned into an almost childish naivete and fear as she watches the scene through the windows of the county superintendent's office. The superintendent himself intimidates her, as his forefinger, "ugly with its ragged black nail and red hairs," searches the map for the place where she is to teach. Her thoughts turn to "hands and fingers she had known back there in Lexington: dried yellow-white fingers of her teachers, her aunt's expressionless too-white hands, brown-yellow fingers of her classmates, and her own. She spread her hands and looked at them as if seeing them for the first time."[1]

This contrast of hands is only one of many contrasts between Louisa's world and that of the mountains. Her studies at the university seem almost absurdly irrelevant in this region "where the ability to ride a mule counted for more than an Einstein's knowledge of trigonometry formulae" (10), and where "illiteracy did not necessarily mean ignorance" (13). Indeed, the locale of her teaching assignment is "a kind of lost place in a bend up Cumberland" (13), where past, present, and future mingle in the melancholy shadows of mountains and trees — a place that, in the minds of its inhabitants, was "made by God Almighty in six days" (12) — a concept that has remained unchanged.

The Cal farm is seen in these same terms of remoteness — almost as if it is the center of a target whose narrowing rings move farther and farther away from the "civilized" world: "The Lee Buck Cal farm lay in a deep twisting valley among steep hills. The valley was so narrow that no sooner did it get down one hill but it must start up another immediately. The farm spread itself upward into the hills on all sides. The log house and barns surrounded by a weed-grown pasture were on one slope, while fields and an apple orchard rose steeply up the first slopes of other hills" (31). Secluded by early-morning fogs and early evening twilights, the farm blends with the nature that surrounds it.

The Cals themselves are attuned to the setting. Their activities, regulated by nature and not by clock time, reflect an easy pragmatism that is foreign to Louisa. When she inquires about the location of the toilet, the answer given is that "We women folks most giner'ly goes up in trees behind the garden" (48). When she worries about what time school should start on the first morning, the response startles her: " 'Don't let th' time worry ye,' Rie consoled after Corie had gone to milk, leaving her and Louisa alone in the kitchen. 'Atter milkin' time an' when we git th' floors swep, an' th' dishes washed, an' us youngens git ready hit'll be school time' " (58). And so it goes throughout the book. Time is not an abstraction, to be measured in hours and days by a watch or a calendar, but something made concrete by a specific activity that is vital to everyday living — from apple picking to corn planting. Thus, life for the Cals is not conceived of in unrelated segments but in one vast continuum.

II. *A Gallery of Characters*

Corie Cal, Lee Buck's wife, is the archetypal mountain woman both physically and mentally. Tall and gaunt and old beyond her years, she views life with a simple and pragmatic fatalism. "Ye ain't very big," she says to Louisa, "but then th' school ain't neither" (35). Corie takes all things as they come, whether it be stirring apple butter, chasing pigs out of the potatoes, or waiting up the whole night for her husband to return from his still. The characterization, which is deftly done, relies not on a sentimental, Mother Hubbardish approach, but on the clearly drawn subtleties of a mountain woman's life that Mrs. Arnow understands so well. Corie has her dignity and her strengths, but she also has her weaknesses. She accepts whatever pleasures or hardships life brings, and she disguises her feelings equally well about either. Her primary concerns are for her man and her children, even to the submergence of her own individuality.

The only times in the book that she shows any emotion are at the prayer meeting and in a conversation with Louisa as they wait for the safe return of Lee Buck and Chris from a dangerous moonshining venture. In the former scene, she is overjoyed when a neighbor, whom she doesn't like, shouts that she has received the spirit, giving Corie a chance to pummel her on the back: "Corie's long web of dark brown hair untangled itself from the pins that sought to hold it, and streamed in a flying cascade behind her shoulders, while her round old hat of a fashion forgotten years before remained jammed on her head with a rakish slant to one eyebrow and an ear, but the condition of her hat and her hair in no way hindered her exertions" (193). In the latter scene, she admits to Louisa that she is worried about the safety of Lee Buck and that she is helpless to do anything about it. This is the only occasion in the novel that her frustration breaks through the wall of fatalism life has fashioned around her:

> "Don't tell me no more. Ye've said too much already. What kin I do, but keep a settin' by th' fire a thinkin' ever' night thet mebbe. . . ." Her voice broke then, and she turned away and looked out the window.
> Louisa would not give up. "You couldn't get Chris to go away, or have Lee Buck quit his work for a while? You know him. . . ."
> Corie looked at her. No longer angry, but with a kind of gentle pity, she thought. "Teacher, I been a raisin' Lee Buck's chillern, an' a cookin', an' a sleepin' uth him fer fourteen yer, but I don't know him well enough tu tell him thet." (317-18)

Lee Buck Cal, farmer, moonshiner, and school trustee, is not so sharply drawn a character as Corie. A moral man in his own way, Lee Buck moonshines because he sees nothing wrong with it. After all, "whiskey was good for snake bites, puney babies, sickly women, weak stomaches, sleeplessness, colds, fevers, fainting fits . . . and helped a person to endure both heat and cold as well as trouble" (131). Lee Buck, patriarch that he is, accepts life and lives it without apology. To Louisa, however, he is somewhat of an enigma. When she is shown a fiddle he has made with little more than a whittling knife, she wonders that he could spend his time thus when gates, outhouses, and steps all needed repair. "Was he," she questions herself, "a shiftless and a no-good or was he merely wise and brave, doing the things he wanted to do because the doing of them gave him more pleasure than firm gates and solid steps could give" (183)? But Lee Buck is also capable of hatred; he hates the Barnetts — enough so to have killed some of their number and to be willing to kill more. He is, Louisa comes to realize, "no different from the rest of the world. The things he hated ruled his life and not the things he loved" (145).

Chris Bledsoe is a mountain example of literature's isolated and doomed young man. A murderer in the eyes of the law, Chris can never fully belong to or feel at ease in the world — even the world of Cal Valley. But he accepts his situation with, "If I hadn't done — what's been done, it wouldn't a been me. There was nothin else" (179). Besides the youngster Rie, he is the person with whom Louisa has the most rapport. She feels that Chris sees the world in the same way she does — with a sensitivity that makes being alive something more than a mere physical process. It is made fairly clear that Chris and Louisa have affection for each other, but Mrs. Arnow deftly handles this aspect of the story, having the good sense not to overdo a potentially trite plot situation. Indeed, the feelings of the pair are never consummated by so much as a kiss. If Chris as a character was added to the story in an effort at developing the narrative line that Strauss suggested was needed when he read the first manuscript, the addition proved successful; for, though Chris is important to the narrative line, his role never impinges in a melodramatic way on the novel's major theme.

Rie Cal, a girl of twelve, is in many respects one of the most interesting characters in the novel. Combining a child's naivete with a woman's wisdom, she is completely at home in her world. The oldest of the living Cal children, she is as much a mother to her younger brother and sister as is Corie. She serves, moreover, as a guide to Louisa, not only in the ways of handling a mountain school but also in many of the more subtle ways of mountain life in general. She is well aware of the trouble in the valley and speaks of the Barnetts in a voice "grown suddenly old with a something less bright and more enduring than the passionate hatred of a child" (168). As a mountain child, she is part of anything that touches her family and nothing is kept from her. There is something pathetic about her, at least from an outside-world view, because, as Louisa realizes, she will become a woman without ever having really been a child: "Rie's waist would twist yet more when she carried her own children instead of her mother's, and the bend of her shoulders grow as she grew with her children, so that at twenty-five, she would be an old woman, never having been a young one. She would know trouble too — vigils by the fire while her children slept behind her and her man was away with other men" (364).

There are, of course, many other characters in the novel — including Samathetie, a kind of nature girl whose primary function is to fill Louisa in on the details of the trouble, and the Gholston woman, who functions in much the same way, with the added twist of being Corie's estranged sister. Because these two characters are obviously manipulated to carry on the narrative, they lack the interest of Corie, Lee Buck, Chris, or Rie. Nevertheless, taken together, all of the novel's characters contribute to a penetrating picture of mountain people and their ways.

III   *Woe, Woe over the Hearthstones*

In the end, however, the main thrust of *Path* lies in the maturation process that Louisa undergoes during her seven months in Cal Valley, for she comes to the valley a girl but leaves it as a woman. "Would she forget a lot in seven months?" she wonders as she listens to the county superintendent outlining her job. The adventure of the situation that she felt back in Lexington quickly gives way to a trepidation and "a violent wishing that it were over" (20). As she moves closer to the Cal farm, first by bus then by mule, the whole setting assumes increasingly an atmosphere of unreality. Yet her progression is not, in fact, toward unreality but toward reality. For, in a very real sense, the world of Cal Valley is an actual world — one uncluttered and unfettered by the complexities of civilization as Louisa has known it. When she sees a gun in the Cal cabin, for example, and comments that she likes guns, her statement shocks Corie, who knows the reality of guns. Louisa had "learned to appreciate a stark beauty in the mathematical laws governing the precision of guns, just as she loved pure science and reason in all things" (44); but Corie knows that guns are ultimately and tragically for killing — a lesson that Louisa soon learns.

This contrast between Louisa and the people of Cal Valley is methodically developed throughout the novel. At the beginning, the young girl feels that she will be able to find a common ground on which to meet these strangers whose difference, she realizes, is not entirely one of education or custom. She has left behind all that is familiar and stable to her, and she must now understand not only the ways of strangers, but also her own reaction to these ways: "Pictures from her long, strange day crowded over her. It seemed as if she had lived not one, but many days since the morning. Yesterday and all the days before yesterday when she had lived in Lexington and gone to school, were too long gone to be measured by time alone" (54-55).

Louisa's world has been one regulated by books and by clock time, a world where "people were tagged and labeled; they were worth so much or had bred so many winners, or had so many letters after their names, or had published so many books, or had spent so many years in research" (124-25). The world she now finds is one regulated by events and seasons — one whose inhabitants are un-lettered but who have a natural dignity that she doesn't completely understand yet respects. She sees that, though in the eyes of the civilized world Chris is an outlaw, he has something in him that goes deeper than written laws. His laws "were of the hill law, older than the modern mechanism of law, rooted in freedom and living people rather than in books" (124). She recognizes that Chris, Lee Buck, and Corie and others of their kind have a basic morality that will not permit them either to steal or to be inhospitable to a guest. That they have a pragmatic side that lets them lie to protect their moonshining operation does not diminish this morality. Such lies, like hate for an enemy, are not seen as wrong by the Cals; they are accepted as a part of life, just as the hills and forests that surround them are.

In Louisa's teaching experience and in her relationships with the Cals, she is made constantly aware of the conflict of values — and, in the process, ironically becomes the student rather than the teacher. Because she is a sensitive girl, the lessons are not lost on her. Her life prior to her coming to Cal Valley had been largely spent in cultivating her mind with little concern for personal relationships and the company of others; but once in the valley she soon wants to know the people and their ways. From Corie, she learns hope and patience, qualities of which she had never before been aware, and gratefulness — for Corie "expected the worst of all possible com-binations in all things, and as a result was eternally grateful for some little thing" (215). From Rie, she learns a simple pragmatism that questions neither hate nor love, neither hardship nor comfort, but accepts them all as they come. From Lee Buck, she learns another lesson in perspective as she watches him move from fiddling to moonshining to killing, remaining all the while a steadfast and moral husband and father. From Chris, she learns of loneliness and love, a love that can never be fully realized.

The pride that Louisa has always had in her own background is shaken by her experience and observations in Cal Valley. Corie, Lee Buck, Rie, Chris — all have an effect on her that eventually forces her to reevaluate her own background and her own goals in life. At first, she retreats to her position of a "sensible person — that is, a chemist with her mind on the future" and tries to put the whole thing out of her mind. "This is not my life," she thinks, "only something I must do before preparing my life" (279). Her whole life to this point has been a preparation for something else yet to come, and she stands in this respect in stark contrast to the Cals. Never content with the present, she has always envisioned a happier time to come — a goal toward which she must work. They, on the other hand, live life in the present and expect it to be no different ever; and Louisa recognizes the contrast. Rie, at twelve years of age, has tasted more deeply of life than she has or perhaps ever will.

Her books, always so important to her, seem diminished in the mountains. She thinks of how she has spent her spare time since coming to Cal Valley:

Long evenings of sitting in the big house while Lee Buck yarned or played his fiddle, bright Saturdays squirrel and rabbit hunting over the hills with Chris and the children, Sundays visiting the neighbors with Corie — Mrs. Hayes Cal's crackling bread and Mrs. Pomp's wild strawberry jam; evenings of possum hunting in the rainy moonlight, other nights of stars and church-going, of cold and sitting by the fire and helping Corie quilt a piece, of shelling corn — there was still a blister from the last time. She saw the pictures of her time, felt them, heard them: the russle of leaves, thud of a mule's feet under her, shouting of preachers, cry of beatle, warm feel of a baby's head against her shoulder, the hardness of Chris's hands when he took her from a mule. And perhaps because these things were brighter than any she had found in books, the feeling of guilt that she might have had a year ago, was lacking now. She had spent her time, and it was gone, and she regretted nothing. (282-83)

Instead of remaining the aloof bystander, Louisa has come to feel "things that she had no right to feel." The statement made by one of her professors at the university, that sentiment has no place in modern civilization and must give way to reason, seems false indeed in Cal Valley. She would break the pattern of her former life and "make of herself a person, an individual with a place in the world of her choosing, not to continue as the docile product and tool of some mechanism of education" (238). But the Cals have no sentiment, and they are products of another kind of mechanism.

Chris, of course, is vital to Louisa's growth from girl to woman, for in him are reflected all the peculiar forces of mountain life. He is a very sensitive person, who, in the city might have been a painter or a writer; but in the mountains — indeed, because of the mountains — he is at best a vengeance killer and at worst a murderer. He tries to escape his situation through a kind of dreaming, but his dreams are not strong enough to shape his life, being constantly pushed aside by the real world of condition. As a hunted man, he must live each day for itself and that in constant watchfulness. Yet, to Louisa's surprise, Chris loves life: "This world must hold the same things for him that it held for her: beauty, and long sad silences, and the play of rain and light and mist over the hills. It oughtn't to. He ought to be insensitive and stupid and un-thinking. It would be easier that way. He had taken another man's life, and because of what he had done he should have lost all love for his own life. Instead, it seemed to her, that he lived with a consciousness of being alive and a love of the life about him more than most men" (178).

Louisa senses the terrible waste in what has happened to Chris. As his name indicates, Chris does indeed bleed, and in that sense he can perhaps be seen as a Christ figure. His sacrifice, however, holds little meaning — certainly none for the Cals, who, though they feel Chris's loss, are totally fatalistic about his death and their surreptitious disposal of his body in the river in the cave. In contrast to the Cals, Louisa has an emotional sensitivity that derives in part from her love for Chris and in part from her rather sheltered background. But, if the Cals' emotions are diminished by their fatalism, Louisa's emotions prevent her from gaining a balanced perspective about the whole affair. She cannot understand their leaving the wounded Chris unattended while they dispose of the bodies of the two men killed by Chris and Lee Buck. She sees their action, not as a necessary protection for the family but as a lack of concern for Chris. But her view, too, is a selfish one, based as it is on her feelings for Chris and on a preconceived set of values that have no relevance in the mountains.

Though she is never fully aware of it, Louisa has moved from observer to participant in the trouble in Cal Valley. Gradual at first, this movement culminates with Chris's death — after which Louisa can coldly wish death upon one of the Barnetts: "Her voice was so smooth and clear, like a stranger's voice. 'I wish,' she said, 'that you would kill him too. He caused it all. He ought to be — in the river — too.' " (372). For the first time in the novel Louisa is alive with true feeling. Her initiation to the realities of life is complete; and, though she vows to leave the valley and "forget them all — dog's eyes — trumpet vine — poplar leaves — and woe, woe, over the hearthstones" (374), the reader is left with the impression that such is not to be. Pencils, pens, and test tubes may enlarge the faint callus on one of her fingers, but they will never erase the indelible print left on her emotions by her experiences in Cal Valley.

Thus, as noted earlier, it is not plot that makes *Mountain Path* a successful novel — for, from that standpoint, the narrative is no more nor no less than those of the host of mountain novels that preceded and accompanied it. Indeed, if *Path* has weaknesses, they lie in the area of plot. Events are melodramatic and often contrived; characters are occasionally incorporated into the story with little or no relevance to the story line; and foreshadowing is often too obvious. But these flaws are diminished when viewed against the total fabric of the novel.

In *Mountain Path* Mrs. Arnow has successfully juxtaposed two life views — that of the inhabitants of Cal Valley and that of the world of "civilization" (Louisa). They bring each other into sharp relief and, indeed, are the *raison d'être* of the novel. In this sense, the plot is merely a vehicle and not an end in itself. Only occasionally does it impinge upon the theme in any obtrusive way. For Mrs. Arnow had the artistic sensitivity and ability to underwrite the story, thus allowing the characters themselves — and the setting — greater exposure. She does not take a moral or ethical stand; she merely presents. But she does not present in a coldly objective fashion as many Realists might.

On the contrary, her sympathy for her characters is clearly discernible. It does not, however, manifest itself in the sentimental fashion that marks so many other mountain novels. Louisa and the Cals all have their faults as well as their virtues. Louisa is in one sense self-centered and narrow-minded; yet, she is a girl with considerable ability for sympathy and understanding. The Cals, hospitable and unselfish, are prone to hate and kill with no more reason than revenge. Living in a world that has no room for sentiment, they are products of a different kind of mechanism from that which Louisa knew in her own world, but one that is just as relentless in its conditioning.

Mountain Path was received with considerable plaudits by reviewers — and rightly so. It represents in Southern-mountain fiction a break with the sentimentalism that marked that genre for so long. A clearly written and neatly structured novel, it is, with regard to its author, indicative of greater achievements ahead; for it indicates her ability to identify with her characters while at the same time maintaining an artistic distance that lets them tell their own story — an ability she sharpened in later fictional efforts.

CHAPTER 3

Four Hill Vignettes

O THER than "The Hunters," an early segment of her second novel *Hunter's Horn,* Harriette Arnow published three short stories prior to the appearance of that novel. Products of a young talent, they are interesting primarily in the hints they provide for work later to come. Both "Marigolds and Mules" and "Washerwoman's Day" dwell simply on themes that Mrs. Arnow works out in more detail and with more artistry in her novels — ones dealing with the struggle of an individual to find meaning and self-identity in a world of condition. These stories, along with "The Hunters," show Mrs. Arnow's ability to remain detached from her material — to permit character and scene to carry the burden. Moreover, they reflect a precision of conception and development that gives them a certain degree of artistic stature in their own right.

I "Marigolds and Mules"

"In "Marigolds and Mules," which was published in 1934,[1] Mrs. Arnow juxtaposes man's love of natural beauty against his hatred of industrial ugliness. Autumn hillsides, yellow with poplar and red with maple, provide a backdrop for the setting of the story — a valley spiked with oil wells and laced with black, snakelike pumping rods that never cease their pulsing rhythms. It is a setting that Mrs. Arnow as a child knew well. The story, marked by a staccato style and a stark brevity, focuses on a single tragic incident. Joe Madigan, a teamster who hauls nitroglycerine needed for drilling projects in the oil field has had to use mules because of the lameness of one of the horses normally used. The roads, moreover, are particularly muddy, increasing the danger for anyone who is hauling high explosives; and Joe, along with his mules, is blown to bits.

Narrated by a nameless young boy, the story presents several points of view regarding life in the oil field in general and Joe

Madigan's demise in particular. Joe himself is never seen in the story, but his wife describes him at the beginning as a man who hates the look and smell of oil but who without fear accepts his lot because "a man must live." In the midst of the ugliness around him he has planted flowers — marigolds — in the yard of his house. "He likes the smell of them after the oil," his wife comments. And on the fated day she picks a bouquet of them for her husband and sends them to him with the narrator so that his father, a driller, can give them to Joe.

Mrs. Madigan is young and, on the surface at least, displays no fear for Joe. "Joe knows how to handle the stuff," she says. "He hauled it in Texas before he came here." The boy's mother, on the other hand, is more conditioned to reality, having lost a young daughter when an oil storage tank exploded. Her reaction to the flowers picked for Joe is a simple "There is no place for flowers. Not here." The exchange she has with her son following his return from Mrs. Madigan's with the flowers underlines her life view and, moreover, is clearly illustrative of Mrs. Arnow's clipped style:

"It will frost tonight," my mother said.
The black snakes by the window went with a long hiss and a rasping growl.
"We'll have a fire," she said.
"Mother," I said, "does Joe bring his load by Big Sinking?"
"Yes," she said. "He has sixty quarts. One horse was lamed. He had to borrow mules. Pete Crowder told me."
She looked at the marigolds. She listened to the rods squeak. "It is good," she said, "there are no children."
"He is not dead," I said.
"No," she said. "He is not dead. But his wife gathers flowers for him before he is home. He drives rough mules. The mud is deep."
"We will saw wood," she said.

Although the narrator's age is never mentioned, references to him by other characters in the story indicate that he is probably somewhere around twelve or thirteen. Like many of Mrs. Arnow's later fictional characters, he is a lover of nature; and he turns to it to escape the man-made ugliness of the oil fields. Just prior to the explosion that kills Joe, he has finished sawing wood and is looking up at a star:

It looked so high. Away up there above the gas and the oil and the dirt. It was a big star, orange red. It made me think of the marigolds. It looked the way they smelled.

The wood was all sawed. I carried it into the house. I made a lot of trips to the woodpile. I wanted to look at the star. If you looked long enough while you stood in the wood smell you could forget the pumping rods, and the gas smell, and the feel of oil in your hair.

He is able, in his innocence, to see beauty in the stars, an ability that experience has robbed from his mother. "You don't belong to look at stars," she advises. And, in one sense, he is about to learn this fact because, following the explosion, he makes both a physical and spiritual journey of initiation to the scene of the tragedy. On the way, he comes upon bloody pieces of mule and one of Joe's hands. It is as if he is descending into a literal as well as a symbolic hell. Indeed, one of the oil men gathered at the scene where the pieces of mule and man are being cast into a fire comments, "Hell will be an oil field." "Hell won't be so bad," the boy replied — and, when asked why, he answers, "There won't be any God damned stars there. . . . Pretty stars to shine on bloody mules and dirty, bloody men." The boy has come face to face with the ironic reality that beauty and ugliness exist together in the world and that the stars shine impersonally on both. The same nature that produces clean-looking stars and fresh-smelling wood also produces the foul-smelling oil and the mud that indirectly kills Joe Madigan. Perhaps the image that shows this duality best is that of a piece of intestine, like a "slimy red garland," decorating a yellow beech tree. Colors that are beautiful and refreshing on one occasion can be ugly and repulsive on another.

II   "A Mess of Pork"

The marginal blurb that accompanies "A Mess of Pork" in *The New Talent,* in 1935,[2] refers to the story as one "filled with latent power, rising to a tremendous and fascinating sweep of horror. A story you will remember." The story does have an element of horror in it, but it is hardly tremendous or fascinating. Artistically, it is not so good as "Marigolds and Mules," primarily because the element of contrivance in it diminishes its power.

"A Mess of Pork" exhibits pretty much the same lean style that "Marigolds and Mules" does; and, like the other tale, it is told by a nameless narrator — this time, a man wanted for killing a policeman. Arriving in Somerset, Kentucky, under the guise of a tax assessor, the narrator learns the location of the cabin of a Mrs.

Fairchild, a widow whose husband Tred was shot by the law for moonshining and left to be eaten by wild hogs. It is not clear whether the narrator was Tred's accomplice who escaped, but Mrs. Fairchild welcomes him to the isolation and protection of her home.

Among the few animals she has on her small farm is a huge black hog to whom she ritualistically feeds fifteen ears of corn each evening. A cannibal hog with teeth sharp enough to devour a man, he is like the ones with whom her husband's body had been left. Her preoccupation with this hog foreshadows that she has something in mind for it other than just butchering it for meat. The narrator soon learns what it is. Mrs. Fairchild, after obtaining the narrator's trust, writes a letter to the two officers that killed her husband, telling them that she knows the whereabouts of the man wanted for killing a policeman. Since they have never seen her and since she uses an assumed name, she is sure that their greed for a thousand-dollar reward will bring them; and it does.

Three weeks later she wakens the narrator early one cold morning, and together they kill the black hog. She then sews pieces of the hog into two pairs of old overalls and wraps another batch of the strong meat in a piece of cloth. Shortly, the two officers arrive and laughingly accept her offer of the overalls as a disguise and the bundle of meat to use as a ruse to get the fugitive to come out of the rock house where she tells them he is hiding. What they find out too late is that she has directed them into a valley of wild hogs from whom even their guns cannot save them. The woman and the narrator look over the edge of a cliff into the valley after they hear shots and the sounds of hogs:

I wanted to look over the edge without being seen. I lay down on the sand rock, and stretched out to look down. I never looked. I heard a man scream. I put my hands over my ears, and pulled my head hard against the rock. Once when I was a boy I saw the brewery stables burn. I remember a big horse screamed and ran back into the fire. Then it screamed again. This scream was like that, and like a woman's. Sometimes I can still hear it. I lay that way a little while, and then everything was still, and I took my hands from my ears and stood up. I listened and I heard them. Their teeth made crunching sounds. The black boar's teeth when he ate the walnuts had sounded that way. I knew there were no walnuts down there.

Technically, "A Mess of Pork" is neatly enough put together — a revenge motif is carefully developed with foreshadowing and suspense, and the ending is a shocking climax. And the story does present a strong character in Mrs. Fairchild, whose motive for vengeance and her strength to carry it out mark her as a kind of forerunner to later Arnow characters who exhibit their own motives and strengths. What is missing in the story, however, is what contributes so much to the rest of Mrs. Arnow's fiction — a deft blending of plot, setting, and character into an artistic whole.

III "Washerwoman's Day"

Of Mrs. Arnow's short stories, "Washerwoman's Day," published in *Southern Review* in 1936,[3] is probably the best. Like "Marigolds and Mules," this story is structured around a single event, the funeral of Clarie Bolin, a poor washerwoman who died from pneumonia because, in order to protect her new shoes, she scrubbed a kitchen floor barefooted. Mrs. Arnow again uses the first-person narrator to tell the story — a young girl named Jane, who is probably around eleven years old.

The story opens with Jane's mother and grandmother discussing Clarie's funeral, which is to be that afternoon. In their opinion Clarie Bolin was an old fool to scrub a kitchen floor barefooted, and they waste little sympathy on her; they worry more about who will now do their washing and cleaning. Forbidden by her mother to attend the funeral, Jane fibs to her teacher that, though she has forgotten the note, she does indeed have permission to attend. With her girl friend Susie, she does go to the funeral, which is being paid for by the Ladies Aid. Indeed, they have sent all the way to Lexington for two dozen white roses for the occasion, a gesture stemming more from their sense of duty than from a sense of compassion.

Clarie Bolin, lying in her coffin, seems to reflect the reality of her life; to Jane, she looks as if she were angry: "I wondered why the dead woman looked the way she did with her teeth clamped tight together and her thin blue lips drawn back a little ways. She looked, I thought, as if she had just come back from a long fight, and had lost the fight. I wished in a dim sort of way that she could know the Ladies Aid had spent three dollars for white roses. I thought it would have made her feel better."

Present also at the funeral is Laurie Mae Bolin, Clarie's daughter. On the pew beside her wrapped in a dirty blanket is her illegitimate baby, fathered, according to gossip, by a man for whom Laurie Mae had worked. Throughout the service she sits staring straight ahead, not crying, not bowing her head during the prayer, and not seeming to notice when the preacher hopes "that the one of the living nearest and dearest to the dead would profit by the affliction that God in His almighty wisdom had seen fit to lay upon her, and change the path of her ways and walk henceforth with uprightness and decency." The Ladies Aid Society decides to give her six of the two dozen roses and to save the rest for their sewing circle the next afternoon. Laurie Mae silently accepts the roses and goes on to the cemetery with the preacher.

Jane and Susie follow the preacher's carriage to the cemetery and expect to see Laurie Mae put the roses on the grave, but she does not. Susie leaves, but Jane hides behind a pillar of the cemetery's gate to see if Laurie Mae, once alone, would cry. She comes out of the gate "and looked around; up and down the road, and at the nearest houses, and up into the snowy sky. When she saw no one she laid the baby on the ground, and took the white roses one by one and threw them in the yellow mud of the road. She pushed them out of sight with her foot and raked the mud over them, and then she picked up the baby."

Clarie Bolin has had her day, but perhaps it is more Laurie Mae's day than her mother's; for though she speaks on but one occasion — when Jane and Susie, after the funeral, ask to see the baby and then tell her that the roses cost three dollars — Laurie Mae is the heroine of the story. But words do not make her the main character; actions do. Her first action of flaunting her illegitimate baby before the Ladies Aid Society is public. Her second action, however, is private and much more symbolic. The first may show her scorn for community mores, but the second shows her defiance not only of man, as it were, but of the entire universe. As she looks around and up into the sky, she does indeed stand alone in a singular testament to her individuality.

IV   "The Hunters"

In 1944, five years prior to the publication of *Hunter's Horn*, Mrs. Arnow published a short story in the *Atlantic* titled "The Hunters,"[4] a story that eventually became a part of the novel. "The Hunters" involves a fox hunt in which Nunn Ballew has been chasing a particular fox for more than six years. Indeed, his old fox hound Zing is considered by the rest of the area's hunters to have the best chance of running the fox down. As in *Horn,* however, Zing is run to death by the fox. Nunn, along with some of his friends, decides to trap the fox in the glare of carbide lamps and then shoot him. Nunn, as the best marksman, is to do the shooting. When he gets the fox in his sights, however, he cannot shoot. The fox's eyes, as Nunn looks into them in the glare of the lights, recall the eyes of a man Nunn had once seen trapped in a coal mine cave-in. He now knows that he must pursue the fox in the true ritual of the hunt no matter what the cost.

Nunn proves to be a variation of nature's nobleman. Surrounded by superstitious and ignorant cronies who do not see the almost poetic ritual of the hunt, Nunn does not hunt for money or to rid himself of a varmint; he does so out of dedication to the hunt as something vital to his reality — something that raises both him and Zing above those around them. Upon this characterization, as well as the basic theme and story line, Mrs. Arnow built *Hunter's Horn.*

CHAPTER 4

Life and Death in Little Smokey Creek

THE artistic promise apparent in *Mountain Path* reached fruition in *Hunter's Horn,* a novel in which Mrs. Arnow once more turned to the Kentucky hills for a setting. If the former work is somewhat encumbered by a melodramatic plot, the latter most certainly is not. In *Horn,* plot, setting, and characterization are woven together in such a way that they reinforce one another. The result is a highly unified and carefully structured story that, coupled with the artistic simplicity with which it is presented, makes *Horn* a novel of considerable distinction.

Covering a period of approximately two and one-half years in the life of the Ballew family, the novel is indeed almost a daily account of that life. Nunnelly Ballew — husband, father, and a fox hunter par excellence — is afflicted with an obsession about hunting down and killing King Devil, a purportedly huge red fox with supernatural attributes that has been plaguing the countryside for a number of years, killing sheep and chickens and leading hounds to their deaths in midnight chases over the treacherous terrain.

In Nunn's quest for King Devil's hide, he neglects his family and his farm to the point that, in one instance, he is forced into moonshining as a way to get some badly needed money. Early in the story, his old hound Zing is led to his death by King Devil; and Nunn takes an oath: "I hope the good Lord God in heaven sends me to brile in hell through eternity without end if I ever stop chasen that fox till I git him. I'll git him if I have to sell ever last sheep I've got to buy me a hound an sell my mare and my cow to feed him. I'll chase him till I'm crippled an blind an bald an . . ."[1] Taking all the money he can scrape together, Nunn buys two pedigreed hound pups, Sam and Vinnie. He nurtures them and trains them in the ways of fox hunting until they finally run down and kill King Devil. Ironically, however, King Devil is not a huge fox: she is a mere vixen heavy with a litter. Stunned, Nunn can only mutter, "He allus seemed big somehow — bigger lots a times than anything else in the world" (490).

With King Devil's death, Nunn gives up fox hunting, selling Sam and Vinnie for 150 dollars in cash and the "awfullest lots a goods I ever seed" (491). While the elation he had thought King Devil's death would bring seems to have eluded him, he is content to have "nothen on my mind but farmen — them hounds a mine, they caught the fox" (491). What appears to be a happy ending, however, is not quite so: for Nunn discovers that his daughter Suse, whose hopes for going to high school were aborted by his being more concerned with fox hunting than with his family, has become pregnant by a young man, Mark Cramer, who has left the area for Detroit. Nunn, shocked and showing little compassion, sends her away to live with her seducer's parents. His wife Milly, though she herself has been trying to convince Suse to go with the Cramers, is upset that Nunn has sent the girl away. She is even more upset when she learns that he has sold the hounds. Nunn can only take solace in King Devil's red shining hide nailed to the wall — the trophy of a hollow triumph indeed. On this sad and ironic note *Horn* ends.

A simple plot summary may leave one with the impression that *Horn* is not much more than a hunting story, a story of men and hounds and the ritual of the hunt. To be sure, the novel is a hunting story; and, as such, it is interesting enough. But that is only the surface of the novel, the threshold, as it were, of a deeper and more poignant story that derives not only from the effects of Nunn's obsession on the characters in the book and indeed on himself but also from the forces that impinge upon the lives of all who live in Little Smokey Creek country.

I   *A World of Solitude and Silence*

Just as in *Path,* the setting is a vital element in *Horn* — even more so because of the increased sharpness with which Mrs. Arnow presents it. Viewed as a series of incidents occurring in Little Smokey Creek country, the novel exhibits many of the characteristics of local color. But *Horn* goes far beyond local color, for Mrs. Arnow is not the kind of Realist who produces merely a photographic and phonographic copy of real life. On the contrary, her Realism exposes the minds of the characters — their fears, their desires, their hates, and their loves. In this process, Mrs. Arnow, as

built a new log cabin around the old chimney, and Preacher Jim had built onto it and — the stone was very hard and very old — it would maybe outlive this house and Lee Roy some day would build a new house, another new house, around the old chimney. Suse's eyes looking into his were young and soft and hopeful.

"Suse," he said, leaning now with both hands behind him, palms pressed against the stone, "I ain't holden th wrong you've done agin you — but this fire — it's never warmed a bastard." (506)

Nunn is unable to break out of the conventional approach to the problem and let Suse stay at home. Ironically engendered in Nunn's victory over the fox then is Suse's defeat, and symbolically and tragically she is nailed to the wall in the same way that King Devil's hide is.

Sue Annie Tiller is one of the most colorful characters in *Horn*. A pragmatic person, she possesses a keen insight into the people and customs of Little Smokey Creek and, moreover, is not averse to commenting freely upon them. She serves not only as a local midwife and unofficial physician but also as a kind of conscience for her neighbors who are constantly concerned lest Sue Annie see them sprouting corn for moonshine, spreading government fertilizer on a potato patch, or eating dried mutton. Unimpressed with superstition and fundamental religion, Sue Annie is a law unto herself and has her own code of action and her own system of values.

When Preacher Samuel rationalizes his not giving Lureenie Cramer credit in his store because he thought she had money, Sue Annie replies, "Next time don't figger so hard ; jist read yer Bible — him that hath two coats give to him that hath none — an don't ask what yer neighbor done with his or why he ain't got any fore you give" (383). And regarding the community's view of Lureenie's death, she comments:

"Looks to me like they's a schism already," Sue Annie said, going to the door to spit. "One bunch a you has got pore Lureenie's soul in hell an one bunch has got her in heaven. You'd all ought to git together an put her someplace fer good ; she had too hard a time on earth, pore soul, to be treated this away after she's dead. If I was God, I'd give her a seat right by my side an give her everthing she wanted." She sighed and looked out across the fields. "But I recken, sean how Rans has got th call, she'll have to go to hell — he'd never have th nerve to meet her face to face in heaven — him with Ruby on his arm." (442)

Beneath her harsh, scolding exterior, Sue Annie is a woman of considerable compassion and concern for her fellow man — a person who, though not always consciously recognized as such by the people, is a source of strength to all of Little Smokey Creek, especially to women and children. She has found her *raison d'être* and accepts it with neither bitterness, frustration, nor resignation, but with an almost fierce pride and confidence in her ability to bring new life into the world and to stand as a protector between the living and the many threats they face from death, even on occasion at the risk of her own life. Yet, she can also accept death without reliance on religion or superstition. When Milly wishes that more people were around when she and Sue Annie are taking care of Lureenie's critically ill children, the latter says, "Shitfire, child, a houseful a people can't keep death out th door — if'n it wants to git in" (379).

Thus, Sue Annie represents in the novel an alternative to the mores of Little Smokey Creek. Like Old Andrew, the schoolteacher who runs his school with little reliance on county regulations, she is concerned more with the actual living of life than with the pretense, self-righteousness, and fear that control the lives of so many of her neighbors.

Through Nunn, Milly, Suse, and Sue Annie, Mrs. Arnow provides four contrasting points of view regarding life on Little Smokey Creek. Nunn recognizes the rude conditions under which he must build a life; but, because his mind cannot grasp their real essence and perhaps because he can do nothing about them anyway, he focuses all his hatred and frustration upon King Devil as a prime cause. And while King Devil lives, Nunn is probably a better, though less wise, man than he is after the fox is dead. As a hunter of King Devil, Nunn is raised to a higher plane than his cronies; but, as a possessor of the fox's hide, his *raison d'être* is gone and with a burst of self-righteousness and pride he can turn on his own daughter.

Milly, on the other hand, accepts her lot with a wistful resignation that severely limits her as an effective force. She never really acts, but merely reacts. Her only moment of what might be called rebellion comes when she learns that Nunn has sold the hounds, but even then her rebuke of her husband is closer to bitter acceptance than real anger. Unlike Milly, Suse refuses to accept the idea that there is no possibility of escaping the grinding pressures of Little

Smokey Creek. She clings to the idea that somewhere beyond the hills are places where one may realize his dreams and capabilities; but, just as pregnancy brings defeat to King Devil, so too does it to Suse. Sue Annie is perhaps the strongest and probably the happiest person in *Horn.* She knows well the limitations of her world, and she faces them with a practicality softened by true compassion. A non-believer to her neighbors, she is the only true believer in the novel. Her actions are based on a generative view of life — a view that does not deny death but accepts it as a part of the whole life process. She sees her function clearly enough and performs it cheerfully and un-stintingly, unmoved by fear of God, devil, or people.

Horn, then, is essentially a novel of people; for it is through its people that the reader comes to a realization and understanding of the novel's theme. To be sure, one could have a time for himself in analyzing the symbolic implications of King Devil, but the fox is not what really holds the book together thematically. Significant, yes, but as a symbol, he is inadequately and only intermittently developed. What does hold *Horn* together is the harmonious blend of plot, setting, and character; and, together, they make the novel a fresh and true picture of Kentucky hill life and of life in general.

Isolated in the backwash of time, *Horn*'s people live out their existence with little hope of bettering their lot or of providing their children with much of a chance to better theirs. The relentless conditions of their world, social and physical, dull their sensitivities and prevent them from experiencing almost any emotion except that drummed up by a ranting fundamental preacher or fired up by moonshine whiskey. As a result, they are driven into a self-centeredness which feeds upon itself, breeding distrust, fear, and occasional violence where there is a desperate need for compassion and sympathy.

In providing this rather devastating view of life, Mrs. Arnow does not resort to involved psychological analysis of character nor to the sentimental or moral pleading of social criticism — though certainly the potential for both is abundantly present in the novel. She presents no heroes, no heroines, no great tragedy. Her people are human, with strengths and weaknesses inextricably bound up in their being profoundly affected by their environment. One anonymous reader, reacting to *Horn,* wrote to Mrs. Arnow, "I bought your book because I thought that any woman with a face like yours would naturally write a book at least clean and uplifting. Your story would have been just as interesting to decent people if you had left out the dirt. Are you a communist? P.S. I am burning your book."[2] Mrs. Arnow, however, was not bent on merely showing the crudeness of Kentucky hill life. Rather, she was writing out of herself about a people and a place that she knows well, achieving in the process a universality that stems from a focusing on the particular.

Thus, while *Horn* is a novel of the soil, it is something more than that. Beginning in the fall and ending in the spring (two and one-half years later), the story is pervaded by a strong life impulse in both man and nature, an impulse that will survive regardless of social or natural barriers. And that is what *Horn* is about. It's not a question of progressing or regressing; it's a question of living or dying — and of the need for love and compassion. Perhaps Herschel Brickell phrased it best when he said of Mrs. Arnow's achievement in *Horn:* "She writes . . . as effortlessly as a bird sings, and the warmth, the beauty, the sadness and the ache of life itself are not even once absent from her pages."[3]

CHAPTER 5

From Kentucky to Detroit City

T HE *Dollmaker,* opening on a remote hillside in Kentucky and closing in a cluttered housing project alley in Detroit, is from beginning to end Gertie Nevels' story, and she as a character looms large. Through Gertie's eyes the reader sees the contrast between life in the Kentucky hills and life in an industrialized city — and, indeed, the disintegration of a family as its members try to make the transition from rural to urban ways. And during the course of the story, it is Gertie who, somewhat like Louisa in *Mountain Path,* gradually comes to a fuller understanding of life in general and of her own life in particular.

Gertie's family consists of her husband Clovis and five children — Clytie, fourteen; Reuben, twelve; Enoch, nine; Cassie, five; and Amos, three. They live on a rented piece of poor land and, like many others around them, have to struggle constantly just to exist. The time is the early 1940's, and World War II is in progress. Nearly all the younger men have been called into the service or have been lured away by well-paying jobs in Northern cities. Clovis, a self-styled mechanic and part-time coal hauler, wants very much to go to Detroit for a job; but Gertie argues against such a course.

Her goal is for the family to have its own piece of land; and, unknown to Clovis, she has been doggedly scrimping for many years to save every cent she can toward the realization of this goal — the Tipton Place, a deserted farm owned by her uncle John. Gertie gets an unexpected windfall when she learns that her brother Henley, killed in the war, has left her his cattle money — some three-hundred dollars. This amount gives her enough money to buy the Tipton Place. Clovis, meanwhile, has been called for his service physical in Cincinnati. He learns that he won't be inducted immediately; but, instead of returning home, he goes on to Detroit and a factory job. Gertie pays her uncle the money for the Tipton Place and sets about with her children to fix it up. Clovis, however, wants her to join him in Detroit. Under pressure from both her mother and uncle, she takes back the money and uses it to take herself and the children to Detroit — and a new life.

In Detroit, the family moves into a small three-bedroom apartment in a housing project called, ironically enough, Merry Hill. Monotonous rows of thin-walled and airless flats, Merry Hill is not only a conglomerate of various nationalities, religions, and social backgrounds but also a strange mixture of prejudice and charity — a place where people turn on each other for seemingly very little reason, yet a place where many of them will come to each other's aid in time of crisis. For the first time, the family comes into contact with installment buying, labor unions, mass education, radio, movies, comic books, and the many other aspects of a complex urban setting.

Clovis is happy enough with their lot, and of the children, Clytie and Enoch learn quickly the ways of the city. Gertie, however, along with Cassie and Reuben, finds adjustment much more difficult. Reuben eventually runs away and returns to his grandparents in Kentucky; and Cassie, in one of the most powerfully evoked scenes in the novel, is killed by a train. Gertie wants desperately to return home, but Clovis having achieved perhaps for the first time in his life, a sense of self-importance will entertain no idea of returning to Kentucky. For awhile Gertie seems to lose all hope, but eventually she realizes that she has no alternative but to make a life for herself and the family in Detroit. The stark facts of debt and Cassie's grave will hold them there. Gertie realizes, too, that all people in Merry Hill have their dreams — their Tipton Places — and that beneath their harsh exteriors lurks the potential for human kindness.

Interwoven throughout the plot is a wood-carving motif that is closely related to the novel's theme. Gertie, like her father, is an inveterate whittler and wood-carver and is extremely skillful in carving everything from ax handles to the tiniest of dolls. Her biggest project, however, is the carving of a figure of Christ out of a huge block of wood, but she is never able to settle on the right kind of face for the figure and ends up splitting the block with an ax, saying, "They was so many would ha done; they's millions an millions a faces plenty fine enough — fer him. . . . Why some a my neighbors down there in th alley — they would ha done."[1] And with that, *The Dollmaker* ends.

I *The Ending of the Beginning*

The first nine chapters of *The Dollmaker* deal with the Nevels family in Kentucky and present a clear picture of Gertie. That she is a woman of considerable strength and determination is evident from the opening episode in which she struggles to get her infant son Amos, ill with diptheria, to a doctor some fifteen to twenty miles away. Riding a mule over muddy hillsides to the nearest highway, she stops an army car carrying an officer and an enlisted man; and, after much pleading and arguing, she literally throws herself and Amos into the backseat. On the way, she deftly performs a primitive tracheotomy on the boy by using her knife, a hairpin, and a poplar bough — and saves his life. Such is the stuff of which Gertie Nevels is made, a woman very much in control of her world.

A large, raw-boned woman with great hands and big-jointed fingers, Gertie has, in addition to physical strength and stamina, keen insight and a questioning mind — characteristics that make her a person apart from most of her neighbors and, indeed, even from her husband Clovis and her mother, both of whom have more in common with each other than with Gertie. In the typical hill tradition, Gertie is a dutiful wife to Clovis: and on one level at least he is appreciative enough. Yet it is clear that he really does not know Gertie. Having been exposed to some of the ways of life beyond the hills, he can smile upon her ignorance of coal furnaces and hamburgers and criticize her disheveled condition when he meets her after her trying trip to the doctor with Amos. Not once in the entire novel, however, does he see through with any clarity the crude exterior to the inner strength and sensitivity that is the real Gertie.

Throughout the story one gets the impression that Gertie's love for Clovis is based more on duty than on need. Certainly while the family is living in Kentucky, she is self-sufficient and has no fear that she will be unable to get along if Clovis is called to join all the other younger men of the community in the service. "I've got to learn to manage this store thout a man," the storekeeper Mrs. Hull says to Gertie. "I keep thinken a man'ull come along when I know they's no man to come" (96). And she watches with envy as Gertie, smiling, lifts a hundred-pound sack of feed lightly to shoulder, saying, "I reckon I'll have to be the man in this settlement" (97).

Gertie's relationship with her mother has never been a close one, and at the time of the story it is perhaps even less so. Mrs. Kendrick, a whining person who holds steadfastly to fundamental religious beliefs, constantly berates Gertie for all manner of sins and weaknesses — from whittling to square dancing (about twenty years earlier) to failing to visit her. Ensconced in a "kingdom of crochet work and potted plants," she stands in stark contrast to Gertie, so much so that they can meet on no common ground physically or spiritually. Indeed, when Gertie is around her mother, she can think of nothing to say and can only twist her hands or pop her knuckles while waiting for the latter to break the silence. In her old home, Gertie feels she is in a "forever alien territory that had from the beginning of her memory made her seem even bigger, uglier, more awkward, more liable to break something than she had seemed in other places" (63). Like the potted plants surrounding her mother that bloom "in a sad, half-hearted way, as if they were tired of the red clay pots, tied with crepe paper, that cramped their roots like too tight shoes" (63), Gertie, in such situations, wants only to escape.

Gertie, moreover, has never accepted her mother's religion. Even as a child she was repulsed by the terrible God pictured by the preacher Battle John Brand:

> His Hell would quiver like the heat waves through the meeting house, and she would sit trying desperately to think of other things, but never succeeding. She could smell her own flesh burning, rising like an incense to God in heaven, with her mother who was forever listening down the golden stairs, but never hearing her daughter cry: "I love Battle John's God. I love the Sunday clothing my poor weakly mother works so hard to make for me."
>
> She never, no matter how hot the coals or bright the flames that Battle John made, was able to say such things, but sat on in sweatyhanded guilt and misery. Was she, like Judas, foreordained to sin, she'd wonder? She knew, but was unable to imagine, that the torture of Hell was a million times worse than the torture of her Sunday clothes. (65)

Gertie's religion is very closely related to her love of nature. Perhaps not a believer in the conventional sense, she nevertheless has a strong religious impulse. She has read the Bible thoroughly and has memorized much of it. But, unlike her mother and many of her neighbors, she does not accept its tenets automatically and unquestioningly. On the contrary, she ponders over passages in an effort to grasp their basic truths and to discover their relevancy to her life. Thus, her religion stems more from her own being than it does from the mouths of shouting preachers like Battle John, "stampeding the souls of his flock to Christ with his twin whips of Hell and God" (65).

With her father, on the other hand, Gertie enjoys an easy relationship that finds its basis in a common understanding and appreciation of the same things, from square dancing to whittling. While her mother would shrink from Gertie's touch, even if it were a gesture of aid, her father when he greets her pulls her tightly against him, whispering, "Gertie, Gertie" (68). Gertie knows her father well — knows that he is the weaker of her parents; and this knowledge makes the Tipton Place, with its proximity to her father's farm, all the more desirable. The loss of Henley has hurt him more, though in a quieter way, than it has Mrs. Kendrick. Both he and Gertie see Henley as having been someone vital and happy who appreciated fully the pleasures of living and working with his hands.

Neither Gertie nor her father believe, as Mrs. Kendrick does, that Henley is burning in hell because he "never found that narrow gate, Lord, that little narrow gate to eternal salvation an life everlasten" (59). Henley, like Gertie, had loved life and saw no wrong in singing and dancing and laughing. He did not, to Gertie's way of thinking, give his life in the war — it was taken from him; and having Battle John pray over him, as her mother desires, will not help. Gertie recognizes that her mother is really concerned only with her own feelings; and, to Clovis's comment that the latter cannot reconcile herself to never meeting Henley in heaven, she replies, "Mom could backslide and go to hell if she's so certain Henley'ull be there" (34).

Gertie, then, cannot accept Henley's death in any kind of a religious framework. In her mind she sees Henley and hears his questions: "Why me? What have I done? Why am I dead? Why?" (48). These are, in one sense, the same questions that Gertie herself has asked from her reading of the Bible. Did Job's children ask why they had to die to test their father's patience? Did Judas ask why it was he who had to fulfill the prophecy? Like Koheleth of Ecclesiastes, from whose writings she on several occasions reads and quotes to her children, Gertie is unable to discern clearly any just plan for man in the world — only a kind of circling monotony. Yet lingering in her mind is the hope that there is, after all, some meaning to life.

Gertie's strength does not derive from a relationship with conventional religion, or with people for that matter, so much as it does from her relationship with nature; for in nature she finds her real sustenance, her point of reference as it were. Indeed, Gertie constantly looks to the stars, particularly the north star, because in finding it, she is somehow able to find herself. It symbolizes for her the freedom and beauty of all of nature — elements so important to her that she is relieved to be told by the doctor tending Amos that her brother Henley, after being mortally wounded in battle, might well have been left by stretcher bearers to die alone outside rather than in a confining hospital tent.

A kind of unconscious Transcendentalist, Gertie likes nothing better than just before dawn to take the clumsy old cedar bucket — "something solid and old, known and proved long ago by hands other than her own" (76) — from her kitchen and go to the spring for water, stopping on the way to look at the morning star and at the spring to take a drink. It is a ritual that connects past, present, and future:

The spring seeped into a hollowed-out basin at the foot of a low ledge, and without being able to see where stone ended and water began she squatted by the pool and dipped the bucket in, then lifted it and drank easily and soundlessly from the great thick rim as others might have sipped from a china cup. The water, cold with faint tastes of earth and iron and moss and the roots of trees, was like other drinks from other springs, the first step upward in the long stairs of the day; everything before it, was night; everything after, day. (76-77)

On another occasion when Cassie asks her mother what is it that makes her always like to look at the stars, Gertie answers,

"Th heavens declare th glory of God; an th firmament showeth his handiwork. Day unto day uttereth speech, and night unto night —"
"But what do they say, Mom?"
Gertie stared up, considering the Little Dipper. "Different things to different people; fer one thing they say, 'We'll never change, an we'll never go away — all the nations on this earth with all their wars, they cain't cut us down like we was trees.' And they say to Cassie Marie, 'Little girl, if'n you lost yer friends an kin you'd still have us an th sun and th moon.' " (117-18)

Gertie has named her last born Amos after the prophet who insisted that God is good and acts not on whim but on principle with justice as His supreme demand. The book of Amos, moreover, closes with the prophecy that the children of Israel will be given their promised land; and it speaks to Gertie in much the same way that the stars do — it offers a fixed source of strength, without the ambiguities of heaven and hell.

Even when she learns that Clovis has not gone to the service but has instead taken a job in Detroit, she does not waver from her goal of obtaining the Tipton Place. She wonders why she and Clovis could not have wanted the same things and why she cannot cry over him as the other women cry over their absent loved ones. But the lure of the Tipton Place is too strong for her to dwell on the sorrow of the war. Later she would "cry for the ones away, look up at God, and quarrel on the why of Henley, who had died with no sin but no salvation" (120). Now, however, she sees the things that "Moses saw when he looked across the mountains to the Promised Land, or that the thief saw when Christ said, 'This day, thou shalt be with me in Paradise' " (121). And, perhaps for the first time, she understands why some people can shout in church. Her foundation, however, "was not God but what God had promised Moses — land" (121).

Gertie, to be sure seeks land as a concrete and visible means of self-fulfillment, and she does so in a conscious and methodical way. She takes great pleasure in pulling the money she had hoarded out of its hiding place in her coat lining and secretly unfolding and counting the bills, remembering where each came from — eggs, chickens, walnuts, molasses. But Gertie has another need burning within her — a need to create; and toward this need her whittling and wood carving are directed. Just as her knife skillfully saves Amos's life, so too does it provide a dimension to Gertie's life that is just as significant to her as that provided by land. For Gertie, good wood to whittle is like good land to cultivate. Both yield their rewards in a direct ratio to the effort and love put into them, and both serve as a vehicle toward an understanding and appreciation of the world.

It is in such a context that Gertie desires to create from the large block of wood her own version of Christ as one who works with his hands and sees nothing wrong with people enjoying themselves. Her problem is to find the right face; for, until she does, the block of wood waits with "only the top of a head, tilted forward a little, bowed, or maybe only looking down, but plainly someone there, crouching, a secret being in the wood, waiting to rise and shed the wood and be done with the hiding" (46). When she sees the Tipton Place almost within her grasp, she feels that she soon will be able to bring the face out — for "the face was plain, the laughing Christ, a Christ for Henley" (77).

Gertie has one more relationship of considerable significance in the first part of the novel, the one with her daughter Cassie. Of all her children, Cassie is the one to whom the mother seems the closest. A youngster of great imagination, Cassie creates Callie Lou, an imaginary companion who is always with her — an extension, as it were, of that part of herself which yearns to be free from the real world of condition that restricts man's freedom. She makes and remakes Callie Lou into whatever she wants her to be, from a child to a grown woman. She even on occasion identifies the block of wood as Callie Lou. Cassie, then, is structuring her world as she wants it, and Callie Lou is her metaphor, much in the same way that the block of wood is Gertie's metaphor. Thus, Cassie and Gertie are very much alike, and the mother understands and accepts her daughter's apparent eccentricities, for "a body's mind couldn't be willed and walled any more than the wind could be willed and walled" (121).

In the first nine chapters of *The Dollmaker,* Mrs. Arnow has skillfully presented a character and a way of life, both of which in the remainder of the novel are tested and redefined by a setting vastly different from the one that has produced them.

II   *There Ain't No Callie Lou*

In Chapter Ten, Gertie joins the migration of Southern hill people to the war plants of Detroit. Jammed with her children into a crowded and foul-smelling train and trying not "to breathe the air that was like a stinking rotten dough pushed up her nose and down her throat" (139), she yearns for the Tipton Place with its clear air and its cedar and pine smells. But Tipton Place and all it has symbolized for Gertie is a receding dream. Instead of the solitude of the stars, trees, and springs that until now have provided her orientation and strength, she now must face the bewildering complexities of urban life — churned as they are by the raw power of a huge industrial machine that clouds the day with smoke and burns the night with white-hot steel as it grinds out tools of destruction.

In describing life in wartime Detroit, Mrs. Arnow is just as successful in evoking a sense of place as she is in describing life in the Kentucky hills. She does not try to picture all of Detroit or even a very large segment of it. Instead, she focuses on an alley in the Merry Hill housing project and makes of it not a microcosm of the city itself so much as a vantage point from which to witness the forces operating in an urban-industrial society as they are manifested in the daily relationships of people living there. Thus, *The Dollmaker*, as do all of Mrs. Arnow's works, tells its story through people; and it is through people that Gertie Nevels redefines her own life view.

Like all rural migrants to the city, Gertie and her family, bombarded by new stimuli from all sides, face the difficult task of adjusting not only to strange physical surroundings but also to even more confusing economic and social forces. Even before she left Kentucky, Gertie was never fully convinced that Detroit was the land of promise that her mother and uncle John pictured and that Clovis wrote about. After her arrival, she knows that it is not. Indeed, her first view of Merry Hill from a taxi window emphasizes the stark contrast between what she has left behind and what she had come to:

... through the twisting, whirling curtain of smoke and snow she saw across a flat stretch of land flame and red boiling smoke above gray shed-like buildings. Closer were smaller smokes and paler lights about black heaps of rock-like stuff strewn over a gray wasteland of rusty iron and railroad tracks. She jumped, Cassie squealed, and even Enoch ducked his head when there came an instant of loud humming, followed by a bone-shattering, stomach-quivering roar. The plane was big, and seemed no higher than the telephone poles as it circled, fighting for altitude. There were several loud pops, but the roar gradually lessened as the plane climbed higher, then was drowned in the clank and roar of the steel mill. (159-60)

If the war disrupts life in the Kentucky hills by taking away most of the men, it disrupts life in Detroit in the opposite way. As Clovis tells Gertie, "They ain't hardly standen room in Detroit" (178). The influx of outsiders lured by well-paying jobs in defense plants puts a strain not only on housing and educational facilities but also on daily human relationships. "Detroit was a good town till da hillbillies come," opines one character. "An den Detroit went tu hell" (302). The alley where the family lives is a world of inescapable personal encounters in which measured responses and degrees of involvement are virtually impossible. It is a continuous tumult of shouting and fighting children and arguing adults. "Yu did trip me, yu dirty lyen son uv a bitch" (236), one child cries. "Go crap on yu mama's neck" (236), another responds. And so it goes, day after day, as diverse backgrounds come together beneath the smoke and the glow of the nearby steel mill.

Much of the social friction has a religious base. The fundamental Protestantism of the hill people clashes with the fundamental Catholicism of the native Detroiters, and the members of each group ironically think that they alone are the true Americans. One hill woman, getting ready to go back home, bitterly comments, "I almost wish I was stayen. I'd help make Detroit into a honest-to-God American town stid uv a place run by Catholic foreigners" (488). Another, speaking of one of her Catholic neighbors, says, "If Christ come knocken on her door, an he couldn't say his beads with a Irish brogue, she wouldn't let him in. If he told about the man with the two coats, she'd call him a communist, and if his beard wasn't blond like the images she'd call him a dirty Jew" (216). Catholic children going to a parochial school jeer at Gertie's children for having to go to a public school with "niggers an Jews an hillbillies" (182), and a Catholic neighbor rebukes Gertie for her speech paterns: "Huh? Youngen, whatcha mean youngen? In Detroit youse gotta learn to speak English, yu big nigger-loven communist hillbilly. Yu gotta behave. I, Joseph Daly, will see to ut yu do. I'm a dacent, respectable, religious good American" (302).

Organized religion in Detroit, however, means as little to Gertie as it had in Kentucky, and she cannot grasp the full significance of the disparaging remarks she hears about Catholics, Protestants, and Jews. On one occasion Clytie scolds her for trying to shop on Good Friday during Tre Ore. "It's when Christ was dyen on the cross," she explains. "They tell yu ove th radio to keep it, an it's somethen yu gotta keep in Detroit or they'll call yu a heathen what never heared a Christ" (369). Gertie's only response is a weary, "I ain't so certain Christ ever heared uv it either" (369). She does come to the realization that Clovis is right when he advises them to talk of things other than religion in Detroit; and, when Enoch asks if it is true that all priests are good and all preachers bad, she says, "We've all got to live together" (460).

While the residents of Merry Hill may disagree about their religious gods, they do not disagree about another kind: the industrial gods — the factory owners, who, from the security of their plush offices and even plusher homes in Grosse Pointe, control the economic destinies of those who work for them. Old man Flint is such a one. Owner of the factory where many from Merry Hill work, he is the object upon which the workers and their families heap many of their hatreds and frustrations at being reduced to mere cogs in an unfeeling, profit-hungry industrial machine. Indeed, when old man Flint dies, there is a general feeling of joy and exultation. "Old man Flint is dead," the children shout, "dead — dead — dead. Old man Flint is dead — dead — dead. Globba — lobba — lobba. Old man Flint is dead, dead, dead; globba, lobba, lob" (499). And the adults, too, call "back and forth across the alley, some wanting to know if the news were indeed true, with others giving joyful confirmation" (500).

Unions, as Clovis points out again and again to Gertie, are the only weapon available to the workers to protect them from excessive production schedules, unfair foremen, and unsafe working conditions. And as such they must be preserved at the expense of dues, meetings, walkouts, strikes, and even blood. Gertie's only answer is that "a body's got a right to be free. They oughtn't to have to belong tu nothen, not even a union" (508). What she doesn't realize, however, is that unions, even with their violence and internal friction, have given the workers something that not even their religions have given them: a tangible sense of security and a feeling of togetherness — precious enough in the dehumanizing world of the industrial machine.

While Gertie does not fully comprehend the many forces that impinge upon those who are part of this industrial machine, she soon recognizes that they tend to prevent people from having any sense of individuality. To be sure, pressures back home militated against individuality, but they were simple and obvious: her mother's nagging, for example, or Battle John's fire and brimstone preaching. In Detroit, however, the pressures are more complicated. "Adjust" is the word used there, but its meanings are as numerous as the various social, religious, economic, and educational institutions that make up a large industrial city. "Yes, adjust," explains a teacher from the school where Gertie enrolls her children; "learn to get along, like it — be like others — learn to want to be like others" (196).

Clovis, despite his at least superficial aversion to the prejudice that surrounds him both at work and in the alley, has adjusted. He is not the thinker that Gertie is, and he tends to accept things as they appear or as they are told to him. "But don't go around talken agin Catholics in this town," he warns Enoch. "It'll git you in trouble quicker'n anything — they's Catholics ever whichaway, seems like. If a body went around talken agin priests an sich, they'd be called a commie" (240). When Enoch asks what a "commie" is, Clovis can give only a vague response and an admonition not to ask questions that could lead him into trouble.

It is clear from the beginning of the novel that Clovis is not so strong as Gertie. He can, for example, barely look at the hole in Amos's neck — the one cut there by Gertie to save the boy's life — when the danger is past and Amos is recovering. And, indeed, Gertie never tells him that it was she who performed the tracheotomy. In Kentucky, Clovis always demanded more of Gertie than he was able to give in return — and deep down he knows this. There he was nothing but a tinkerer who picked up odd jobs where he could. In Detroit, however, he is a machine repairman and makes good money.

And he does learn to want to be like others. He readily falls into the pattern of buying on time, scolding Gertie when she wants to save money: "Save . . . That's all I've heard since we've been married. Cain't you git it into yer head that millions an millions a people that makes a heap more money that I'll ever make don't save? They buy everything on time. They ain't starven their youngens" (258). When she yearns for more space in which to live, he snaps, "Millions a youngens that has growed up in furnished rooms three floors up ud think a place like this with room fer youngens to play outside an automatic hot water an good furniture was heaven" (258). Clovis's idea of heaven is quite different from Gertie's.

The impact of the city is felt in different ways by the children. Clytie and Enoch, and even little Amos, adjust readily enough; but, as noted earlier, Reuben and Cassie do not. Either way, Gertie sees the family slipping away from her and indeed from one another. Clytie becomes enraptured by the daily radio soap operas, listening to "tearful declarations of love, long amorous sighs, mysterious rustlings, wicked, forever wicked mothers-in-law, brassy-voiced villainesses, sobbing misunderstood wives, and noble cheated upon husbands" (315) and to commercials in which husky-voiced men croon about the beautiful body Clytie will have if she uses a certain bath soap, "until her eyes softened, glinted, and her lips moistened as she twisted her head about to consider the beauties of her arms and legs" (315). But she learns, too, the realities of urban life: to stay away, for example, from strange men who offer rides to high school girls. She takes great glee in recounting to Gertie how she and her girl friends have foiled such attempts — "Yu gotta treat um that way, jist like Clare Bodell on u radio" (498).

Enoch, too, who relishes all the excitement — the games, the arguments, the fights — of the alley, develops a kind of youthful cynicism. On the taxi ride from the train station to Merry Hill, he innocently describes to the driver the second reader's idealistic version of policemen and their duties. Later, when Gertie suggests that perhaps someday Enoch could be a policeman, he replies, "Who wantsa be a cop? They don't make no money, less'n they've got a beat where they can git shakedowns like a feller Jimmy Daly's pop knows" (549). When Gertie questions Amos about his recollection of things back home — trees, the spring, the dog Gyp — his response is "Huh?" Then a train goes by with a roar that jars the whole house, and Amos, listening and smiling, says, "That train carries people." Gertie turns away with "You're a learnen your trains, son" (246).

Reuben is a different matter. Silent and sullen, he has never forgiven Gertie for bringing them to Detroit, and all that happens to him there merely underscores his resentment. "I ain't maken myself over fer Detroit" (305), he says to Gertie. She understands what he feels; indeed, she feels the same way. But in her attempts to adjust and to help him adjust, she builds the wall between them higher — until real communication is impossible. When she says to "try harder to be like th rest — tu run with th rest — it's easier, an you'll be happier in the end — I guess" (329), she doesn't really believe it herself because she knows that, just as she could never accept her mother's and Battle John's God, neither can Reuben accept what he sees as an artificial and meaningless existence. "But he cain't hep th way he's made," she says to one of his teachers who complains that he just won't adjust. "It's a lot more trouble to roll out steel — an make it like you want it — than it is biscuit dough" (324). And that she does believe. Thus, when Reuben leaves, Gertie understands why he must return to Kentucky, and beneath her sorrow at losing him lurks a secret envy at his determination to remain an individual. But she also recognizes an ironic reality in Reuben's absence, a reality that has its source in the very nature of city life:

She missed him, but could never tell him how she missed him most. She hated herself when she lied, trying to make herself believe she missed him the way a mother ought to miss a child. In the old song ballads mothers cried, looking at tables with empty plates and rooms with empty beds. But how could a body weep over a table where, even with one gone, there was yet hardly room for those remaining. The gas pipes were still overcrowded with drying clothes; and eight quarts of milk instead of ten in the Icy Heart meant only less crowding, not vacant space. Two pounds of hamburger cost less than two and a half, and — She would hate herself for thinking of the money saved, and try never to think that living was easier with no child sleeping in the little living room. (357)

Little Cassie — here is the most poignant story of all. Not feeling at home in Detroit like Clytie and Enoch and not openly defying it like Reuben, Cassie always seems "like child away from home" (199). Cassie tries to keep Callie Lou alive in Detroit, but the other children in the alley ridicule her, pointing to their heads and shouting, "Nuts ina bean, hillbilly" (366). Even Gertie eventually scolds her for talking to Callie Lou: "You know well as I do you're talken to yerself. There ain't no Callie Lou" (366). Too late, Gertie recognizes the mistake she has made — that she has forgotten what she told a neighbor woman who liked to paint: "Don't quit . . . Everybody needs a little foolishness" (245-46). So Cassie, searching for a place for herself and Callie Lou, is run over by a box car being shunted by a switch engine and dies in Gertie's arms:

> Cassie must smile. She must lift her head and know that there was Callie Lou. But Cassie, shivering like one freezing, struggled with some mighty effort to speak, spoke at last, her voice a low gasp of terror, the pupils of her eyes were big, so big they almost covered the lights and freckles in the dark brown eyes — greedy the pupils were for light and seeing — "I cain't see, Mom — s' dark." The eyes were widening, straining.
> "It's dark — real dark," Gertie said, "but even in the dark you can see Callie Lou" (394).

Thus, the family that was so tightly knit in Kentucky is splintering under the impact of the changing images and sharp discontinuity of city life — and particularly by the need to adjust. As she did when her brother Henley was killed, Gertie searches for some meaning behind everything that has happened. But all she can think of are Job's words: "For there is hope of a tree, if it be cut down, that it will sprout again, and that the tender branch thereof will not cease . . . But man dieth, and is laid low . . . and the river wasteth and drieth up: so man lieth down, and riseth not" (428). Through a pink haze of phenobarbitol she chases the flitting image of Callie Lou and dreams of "earth and trees and hills and running water" (429). Her basic strength, however, reasserts itself. She realizes that the pink medicine may take away the anger and hate she feels, but it will also take her individuality. So she turns to everyday tasks: "I'll never git my strength back a layen in bed — an already I'm so behind in everthing I never will git caught up" (437).

III   *Faces Enough*

To be herself, always so important to Gertie, is not easy in Detroit. The values that sustained her over the years in Kentucky were rooted in a right relationship with nature, a relationship that is virtually impossible to realize in a housing project where there are no trees, where the stars are obscured by smoke, and where time, instead of being "shaped by the needs of the land and the animals swinging through the seasons" (199), is measured by ticking clocks and screeching whistles. In Kentucky, Gertie was her own woman; but, more than that, she was the force that held her family together. She knew her husband and each of her children — their strengths, their weaknesses, and their dreams.

Moreover, she knew her own dream — to own the Tipton Place; and, though she might have wondered in Kentucky just as she does in Detroit about the ultimate meaning of life, she always had that dream to sustain her. In Detroit, however, she must find something else for spiritual sustenance; and, when she does, she becomes more than she was in Kentucky.

In Detroit, as in Kentucky, Gertie's wood carving serves as a metaphor for her search for order and permanency. But she is not to find them through carving alone, just as she would never have found them through land alone. Gertie learns this lesson from the people in the alley: from Max, who needs a dream to get her through each day, who finally leaves her husband to try to make dreams into reality, and who bids Gertie goodbye with an awkward kiss on the jaw and the words, "I wish you'd been my kin" (446). From Mrs. Anderson, who also wonders on the meaning of life: "But sometimes I wonder — why raise children? Why give your life up to them — everything — if — if their lives will be as miserable as your own? Why?" (423). From Mrs. Daly, who brutally throws a bucket of soapy water on a woman spreading God's word in the alley, yet who says to Gertie, following the dropping of the atomic bomb.

"Yu gotta realize that it ain't like them Japs was good white Christians; as Mr. Daly says, them Japs is pretty near as bad as them communist Russians — but," and she looked about her and spoke softly, guiltily, as if her words were treason, "yu still gotta say, people is people. Why them Japs lives something like this," and she waved her hand over the flowers, the low houses, the child-flooded alleys, the babies, "all crowded up together ince towns; little cardboard houses kinda like what we've got; and maybe lotsa — you know — kids." (476)

From all who show her the "bigness of the alley, the kindness; big enough and more it would have been for Callie Lou — and maybe Reuben, too, for the alley and the people in it were bigger than Detroit" (420).

Thus, Gertie comes to understand and appreciate people — something that she could never have fully come to in the hills. But, more than that, she learns something about herself and the Christ that she has been seeking for so long. Before, she could bring him alive only in her mind, like Cassie with Callie Lou; in Detroit, she brings him alive through her experiences with people. She also realizes that He has not one but many faces. In her final symbolic act of splitting the block of wood, she does not destroy her Christ, but brings him alive — for He cannot be abstracted or fixed; He must live in people.

Using her knowledge of the Kentucky hill people and of life in a war-time Detroit housing project, Mrs. Arnow presents in *The Dollmaker* a realistic story of human aspirations and tragedies. Though it is a rather long novel, it still maintains the pace that marks all of her work. To report so many daily events, as Mrs. Arnow does in *The Dollmaker,* could become dreary indeed; but such is not the case. Through careful selection and skillful weaving, she brings these events together in a thematic unity that holds the reader without any melodramatic surprises or sentimental intrusions. Moreover, she has successfully resisted the obvious temptation that such a story offers for moralizing. While she may deplore the conditions that limit man, she never once condemns man. Nor does she distort her characters to achieve tragedy; or to put it another way, her characters are not pathetic but human. Along with *Hunter's Horn, The Dollmaker,* then, represents the best of Mrs. Arnow's literary efforts.

CHAPTER 6

Pioneering on the Cumberland

T HAT Harriette Arnow should have turned to writing about the Cumberland River basin in a factual way is not so strange when one remembers how much a part of her life that area has always been. The roots of *Seedtime on the Cumberland* (1960) and *Flowering of the Cumberland* (1963) go back to Mrs. Arnow's childhood when she listened intently to the plethora of stories told by her parents and grandparents and when she wandered alone over the hills and valleys near Burnside. For, in one sense, that is when her research for these two books began. Perhaps at that early age much of the lore and many of the facts about the Cumberland were unconsciously catalogued in her mind, but no one can deny that over the ensuing years Mrs. Arnow, by "poking and prying and wandering," has gleaned a wealth of information about the land and its people and, moreover, organized it into two excellent examples of social history.

I *Conquering an Environment*

In the acknowledgements of *Seedtime on the Cumberland* Mrs. Arnow states that the book is not a history, "nor is it concerned with the lives of famous men and women, nor does it pretend to be an exhaustive study of the pioneer. I have tried to re-create a few of the more important aspects of pioneer life as it was lived on the Cumberland by ordinary men and women."[1] *Seedtime* may not be a history in the formal sense, but it is certainly made up of the stuff of history. Drawing not only upon her own rich background, Mrs. Arnow delved deeply into state records, county court minutes, wills, deeds, diaries, letters, and the important Lyman Draper manuscript collection for her material — material which she has ordered into what Donald Davidson described in a review as a kind of grand historical scrapbook.[2] And, because it resembles a scrapbook, *Seed-*

time captures the imagination of the reader in a way that most histories, social or otherwise, do not. As Mrs. Arnow says at the end of the first chapter,

How was it then, life on the Cumberland before 1803 when "We" bought the Louisiana Country, before men were split by The War with Middle Tennessee one world and our part of the river there. I wondered but never found a book. A very great deal has been written — histories, the lives of famous men associated with the region — Andrew Jackson, Sam Houston, Davy Crockett, Sergeant York, Cordell Hull, President Polk, famous jurists and lawyers, generals and admirals, and of course the most notorious of all criminals, the Harpers. Other writers have dealt in detail with the famous roads that crossed the river — the Natchez Trace and the Wilderness Road — and many works of fiction have used some segment of the country as background, but almost nothing has been written of the actual life of the first settlers, the why and the how of the ordinary people who came first to the Bluegrass and the limeston valleys. (18)

Divided into fourteen chapters, all fairly long, *Seedtime* opens with a more-or-less personal reminiscence of Mrs. Arnow's childhood home on the Cumberland — a reminiscence that establishes a definite sense of place in the mind of the reader. The "old boot," as she refers to the 325-mile drainage basin of the Cumberland, hooks down from eastern Kentucky into middle Tennessee and back up again into western Kentucky in a "shoe-like shape, something like an old-time buskin, badly worn and wrinkled, with a gob of mud caught in the instep" (13). Train whistles have replaced steamboat whistles, and roads have opened up travel throughout the area, but for many years the river was vital not only as a source of water but also as a means of transportation and communication. As often as not the main topic of conversation during those years, the river provided rich material for storytellers; and the tales, which ranged from baptisms to those of "weddings, births, deaths, funerals, the news, and the mail, all hedged about the rising creeks with overturned buggies and swimming horses" (11), have been handed down from one generation to another.

The river was not the only bond connecting the people of that section of the country. Indeed, the great majority of settlers came from the same general areas — Virginia, North Carolina, and eastern Tennessee — and "most of us," writes Mrs. Arnow, "had more kin southward in all directions than north or east in Kentucky and

Tennessee; the Cumberland Presbytery, for example, was organized according to the river, not state boundaries" (16). And all could boast of at least a few ancestors who had fought in the Revolution.

The love of land was another bond among these people of the Cumberland; and farming, more than a mere occupation, "was a way of life that colored all our days from birth till death with family food coming directly from the land or the products of the land" (8). Among the crops grown were almost all of those known in the New World. While cotton was once a chief cash crop, Mrs. Arnow is quick to point out that, unlike in the deeper South, cotton was not king, "for the Cumberland would never have a king, not even Andrew Jackson" (9). Nor was the land king. Important as it was, it never overshadowed the water; for, if land was not watered by the Cumberland itself, it was by a creek or branch that was fed by or drained into the river. Even place names, if they had no relationship to water, faded into the background; and people "were born and were buried, not in the half-remembered names of non-existent places that were names only, thought up to make the exchange of mail possible, but on creeks and branches" (10).

Using her childhood as a springboard, Mrs. Arnow jumps back in time to the early geological ages of the Cumberland, tracing its development from the Paleozoic era when the whole area was a vast sea to the time of the first settlers. Not averse to even quite steep slopes, these settlers found in the Cumberland basin a variety of soils, plenty of water, and limestone and sandstone for various uses, all the way from chimney mortar to millstones. Farming to them was a way of life, not merely a capitalistic enterprise; and they "welcomed this land that offered so much in addition to rich soil; they were blind to nothing; a small waterfall up a rocky creek could mean a mill; and a scantily soiled limestone ledge, unfit for any cultivated crop, was a thing every settlement needed; such places were almost invariably thick with red cedar, and cedar was a must for churns, pails, and piggens" (39).

Prior to these settlers, however, were other peoples; and Mrs. Arnow speculates about the various ways of life that must have been represented through the centuries along the Cumberland. Burial grounds, skulls, pottery, and artifacts of all kinds have been uncovered in the area, enabling such investigators as W. E. Myer to learn much about prehistoric inhabitants. But as interesting as such early groups are, it is with later groups that the primary interest of

Seedtime lies — the early French explorers and trappers, the "Shirt-tail Men," "The Travelers," and "The Woodsmen."

In writing of these groups, Mrs. Arnow avoids romantic stereotypes. Relying on a detailed description of their everyday activities, she brings them alive with an objectivity and a freshness that raises *Seedtime* to a level of drama usually found only in fiction. The personalities are legion and colorful: the Frenchman Martin Chartier, a Canadian who went south not for material wealth, but for the love of an Indian woman, and who spent many years wandering over the Cumberland area, hunting, fishing, and living with the Indians; the ballad maker James Smith, whose ability to survive hardship and danger in the wilderness enabled him to become the first man "to leave a fairly clear record of men who went from the English colonies across country to the lower Cumberland" (138); the Cherokee half-chief Attakullakulla, who, though small of stature, tirelessly strove to keep peace between the Cherokee and the English because he believed that "One God is father of us all" (179); the able woodsman Kaspar Mansker, who "was the first actual settler in Middle Tennessee" (241); teenager Nancy Gower, who, though wounded by an Indian bullet, guided a boat to safety after the men ran off; and schoolmaster Zacharia White, who interrupted recitations to help repel an Indian attack and in the process was mortally wounded — to mention only a few.

While the gallery of personalities Mrs. Arnow presents in *Seedtime* gives the book a dramatic quality, the detailed descriptions in the last three chapters of the everyday activities of the pioneers give it a realistic quality. In what Davidson referred to as some of her finest writing, Mrs. Arnow in these chapters discusses everything from washtubs, beds, and women's underclothing to cabin building, soap making, and butchering. And she reminds the reader in doing so that these were indeed real people with all the attendant strengths and weaknesses that mark the human condition. They did not, as some historians would maintain, invent democracy or pioneer a new system of government, religion, or agriculture. On the contrary, those that survived did so because they were masters of adaptation. Nor did they, as far as Mrs. Arnow is concerned, possess a peculiar "pioneer mind":

Much has been written of a thing called "the pioneer mind." I found no mind I could hold up and call the "pioneer mind," and no man I could call "the pioneer." The difference between the first settlers on the Cumberland and the rest of the country was one of degree and not of kind. They did not call themselves pioneers; later, other men, viewing them with different eyes, gave them the name. The bold ones lived to learn they were the last of their generations to plant British culture in the woods. Past the Mississippi the trees thinned, and the settlers who went there were quite often self-consciously American. Whatever the pioneer on the Cumberland was, he was not that. As one delves deeper into the complexities of his social, intellectual, and educational life one realizes more and more that the purely physical aspects of his world were in a sense the least of him. One also realizes there can never be a complete and perfect seeing. We cannot see him as he saw himself; this is not a mere matter of time or change in physical environment. Our eyes, looking at him across the years, must study him through a maze of modern concepts in sociology and psychology, unknown to the pioneer, but thick about us as Cumberland River fog. Our attitudes toward religion, man's relationship to his government and his fellow man are entirely different from those that surrounded the old south from which most pioneers came. Pavlov's dog had not yet salivated, and the Reformation was still a vital force. (427)

II *At Home on the Cumberland*

Picking up where the last three chapters of *Seedtime* leave off, *Flowering of the Cumberland* is not so much a sequel to the former as it is a companion piece — dealing with the same general period, 1780 to 1803. In the Introduction, Mrs. Arnow points out that *Flowering* contains less of great events and famous men than does *Seedtime* — that it "is concerned with the pioneer as a member of society engaged in those activities which, different from hunting or house building, could not be performed by a lone man or family."[3] *Flowering,* then, is indeed a social history, as a sampling of its chapter titles indicates: "The Makeup of Society," "The Sounds of Humankind," "Intellectual Background and Education," "Industry," "The Professions," and "Social Life and Diversions."

The book opens dramatically enough as Mrs. Arnow describes an Indian attack on a fort along the middle Cumberland. The station, referred to as Buchanan's, included eight families living in small log houses surrounded by picketed walls with a blockhouse at each corner. No one particularly liked the confinement of fort life, but it was necessary as a protection against Indians. And many of those that rejected it wound up dead or ruined financially. Sally Buchanan, for example, whose husband Major John Buchanan was one of the early settlers on the Cumberland, had no recollection of a time or place safe from Indians. Life along the Cumberland was not an easy one. "The wonder," comments Mrs. Arnow, "is not that in 1792, close to thirteen years after the beginnings of settlement, there were only seven thousand settlers in one of the most fertile regions on earth, but that there were any at all" (12). Far from Rousseau's noble savages, the Indians as described by Mrs. Arnow were thieving, scalp-hunting marauders who often left in their wake "eternally maimed, massacred, dispossessed settlers who wanted troops, ammunition, help against the Indians" (13) — things that the government in Philadelphia was not always too quick to provide.

The seige of Buchanan's is remembered as one of the bloodiest battles in the history of Tennessee. Surprising the fort early one morning were "a screaming, howling flood of painted Indian warriors, no mob, but a determined organized army of around four hundred of the flower of the Creek and the Chickamauga, led by the wiliest chiefs who ever lived" (25). Only seventeen men were defending the fort, but they succeeded in defeating the Indians — helped in no small degree by pregnant Sally Buchanan, who, with a bottle of whiskey in one hand and an apron full of bullets, went her rounds supplying and cheering the defenders; and by Jemmy O'Connor, an Irishman who, though inexperienced in firing guns, broke the Indians' spirit with a tremendous blast from an old blunderbuss that sent down from his blockhouse perch "a death-dealing sheet of flame and bullets, cannonlike and devastating. The blood-hungry scalp cries of a moment before changed into howls of fear and pain. The ring of faces by the walls swiftly became backs, receding, leaving wounded and dead" (28).

Sally Buchanan was only one of many pioneer women who provided the "underpinning" for the Cumberland settlements. There was no real debate regarding the place of women in the Cumberland, "for her place like everything else in life 'all depended' " (36). Women were regarded as yoke mates and individuals, and indeed they were. One Mrs. Wilson, for example, threatened to cut off the hand of a government official who was trying to impress her horse. When shown a warrant from the governor, she remarked that the governor could "kiss her arse" (37). Such a comment is perhaps not so surprising in view of the great responsibilities women had in running homes on the frontier. Men were often gone for such reasons as business, political matters, hunting, and Indian fighting; and the women had to be self-sufficient. As wives, they were partners in the institution that most certainly did form the foundation upon which all life along the Cumberland rested.

In 1795, there were, according to Mrs. Arnow's figures, close to six thousand children in the Cumberland area — an attestation to the stamina and perseverance of the women, for child bearing was no easy matter and the infant mortality rate was high. In speculating about these children, Mrs. Arnow sees them as having been

smaller, livlier, thinner-faced than are the children of today; soft roundness there may have been in some past babyhood, but I see them as big-toothed little girls with thin cheeks and big eyes; boys, shy and scrawny, growing sometimes into scrawny, thin-fleshed men, and all, if the old portraits of their elders be anything to judge by, with more of nose and chin and mouth and eye than the average American has today, their faces less flat and more animated, for chance accounts indicate the pioneer child was gigglesome, restless, forever singing or shouting or racing about when not studying or working. (85)

Predominantly of Scotch-Irish, Scottish, and English backgrounds, the settlers had a common cultural heritage. But the frontier environment itself provided the strongest bond among them, for they all knew hardship and danger, log houses and farming. And they all knew the land and its wonders:

Few places on earth have ever held so much of beauty and of wonder as did the varied lands of hills, never too high for a boy's climbing, caves, sinkholes, creeks, waterfalls, glades, meadows, and stretches of heavily timbered land along the Cumberland. The trip to county court, the ride to mill, or even the walk to school was through a constantly changing world that held something of interest and often of value — chestnuts, an unusually fine arrowhead washed into the gullied road, a swan on the river — for rich and poor alike. (89)

Despite all that the Cumberlanders had in common, Middle Tennessee, Mrs. Arnow is quick to point out, was never one "big happy family"; but those who remembered the confinement and togetherness of fort life had learned to live with one another — "not through any attempt to make each like the other, for no place had such a diversity of human beings, but through an awareness that men were different" (163). Social distinctions, however, were present and were clearly understood. Most of the political leaders in Tennessee, for example, were well-to-do members of families that were important in colonial affairs before the Revolution. Even Andrew Jackson, that political archetype of the common man, was put into office and kept there by men of means.

One of the more interesting of the book's chapters is that titled "The Sounds of Humankind." In it Mrs. Arnow discusses the language of the Cumberlanders, who, she points out, were a talkative people. More than a mere means of communication, their language was an intimate expression of their personalities, and never did they pass up an opportunity to use it. In the world of the Cumberland, "where nothing was standardized, nothing could be taken for granted, everything in process of rapid change, work done by human beings and animals instead of machines, and the whole accomplished by many-sided men and women who shared continuously in the lives of others — everything from helping bring a baby to taking a flatboat down river with the baby's father — there was a constant need of conversation" (130).

As one might expect, many words bore a direct relationship to the land — not only administrative terms like "squatter," "land office," and "entry taker," but also names for geographic phenomena such as "river bottom," "sidling pass," "sinkhole," and "bluff." The prevalence of guns and their frequent use gave rise to expressions like "hold your fire," "flash in the pan," "keep your powder dry," and "the biggest bullet doesn't always make the most noise." Government, amusements, eating habits, farm chores — all contributed to a vocabulary that was chosen not for beauty but for clarity. The Cumberlanders "lived in a world that held bellies, bottoms, guts, and not infrequently 'arses.' People puked and belched, and in general said what they had to say in the clearest possible way" (143).

And so it goes throughout *Flowering,* as Mrs. Arnow dwells on all aspects of the life of the early settlers along the Cumberland. The reader learns not only about such broad areas as language patterns, social structures, religious views, farming methods, educational efforts, river navigation, and business endeavors, but also about songs sung, jokes told, and games played.

It is, to be sure, always dangerous to generalize about any group of people, the Cumberland pioneers notwithstanding; and Mrs. Arnow does little of it in either *Seedtime* or *Flowering.* In neither does she attempt any definitive social, intellectual, or political theory; she merely lets the wealth of detail she had at her disposal speak for itself. The result is two books that present clearly and unsentimentally a way of life that is as refreshing to the reader as it was hard to the Cumberlander. In short, *Seedtime* and *Flowering* provide one of the best pictures of what life really was in the "old boot."

CHAPTER 7

A Child of Modern America

MANY of the characters in Harriette Arnow's novels are involved in a quest of one kind or another. Louisa Sheridan in *Mountain Path* embarks on an unconscious search for maturity and an understanding of herself; Nunn Ballew in *Hunter's Horn* seeks self-fulfillment in his chase of King Devil; Suse Ballew in the same novel yearns for an escape from the crude moral and social milieu in which she is trapped; and Gertie Nevels in *The Dollmaker* searches for a face for her carving of Christ. Susie Schnitzer, the main character in *The Weedkiller's Daughter,* is no different. A precocious fifteen-year-old girl from Eden Hills, an elite Detroit suburb, she strives to realize an ideal — one engendered in a preservation of her own self-identity.

Coming from a contemporary background of considerable affluence, Susie, on the surface, is a dutiful and loving daughter. In reality, however, she is an outcast; she is unable and unwilling to fit into the pattern of living prescribed generally by Eden Hills and specifically by her politically and socially right-wing father. Living in the computer age, she has ironically programmed herself — with her own internal computer, TV, and radar — to react to any given situation in the way expected by the Establishment. She is well aware of the roles one is required to play; but, unlike her parents, she will not let these roles become her reality.

Thus, until she is old enough to realize her goal of emigrating to Canada on her own, she must resort to lies and tricks to insure the integrity of her identity — doing such things as keeping up a clandestine relationship with her maternal grandmother, who caused a "civil war" in the family when she was accused of un-American activities — activities that to Susie were only "attempts to help people not much of anybody else would help: like Sacco and Vanzetti a long time ago, and refugees from Franco's Spain, and the interned

Japanese in World War II, and the people wrecked by un-American investigations";[1] attacking her father's weedkilling campaign with anonymous letters to the newspaper; maintaining a hidden flower garden despite her father's aversion to anything resembling a living flower; and hiding her cousin Ter after he, in a melodramatic effort at doing something significant, robs a bank.

Seen entirely through the eyes of Susie, the novel is primarily concerned with her and the small group of school friends who see things in much the same way she does: Robert, whom she dates, even though he is closer to The Establishment than any of the others; Iggy, who lives with his mother and stepfather and who must surreptitiously arrange to visit his artist father; Katy, a talented flutist whose father's career is being threatened by right-wing forces; Angus, fiercely independent son of an Establishment-type minister; and Ben, a Negro boy whose gentle self-assurance impresses Susie.

If there is a climax in the novel, it comes at the end when Susie goes for the last time to talk with a neophyte psychologist who has been interviewing a group of students from her school for a study in depth of alienation. Susie has been chosen for the study because of some scars around her head received in a childhood accident. Throughout the story, Susie has been dreading this interview for fear that the psychologist will learn that she is not the normal American girl fitting into a mold prescribed by the adult world. In an interestingly written episode, however, she outwits him and leaves the interview knowing that she hasn't given away any of her secrets.

I   *A Little Dove in a Nest of Hawks*

In both *Hunter's Horn* and *The Dollmaker* a breakdown in communication occurs between parents and children — and so too is there one in *The Weedkiller's Daughter,* but this one is accompanied by an apparent lack of love. Although Nunn Ballew of *Hunter's Horn* may not fully understand Suse, he does have love for her, and she for him; and the same is true in the case of Gertie and Reuben in *The Dollmaker.* The situation between Susie Schnitzer and her parents, however, is different. Conditioned by a materialistic world where appearance is all important, where new money tries to get close to old money, where old money tries to maintain its position of superior isolation, and where prejudice and discrimination abound, Mr. and Mrs. Herman Schnitzer seem almost incapable of love. Whatever potential they may have had for basic human emotions,

ideals, and relationships have been suffocated among the carefully
groomed two-acre executive estates that symbolically dot Eden Hills
— houses sitting on "browning grass, much of it so lately laid the
seams still showed, some of it dead, as were several shrubs standing
brown and crisped. Even the planting of small things, though green,
stood as if making up their minds to grow or die, for each said: 'I
was once alive and so don't belong here.' The swimming pools of
many different shapes, but all of the same hard bright blue that had
nothing to do with the sky, had an 'in' look. They had never been
alive" (58).

Even more symbolic of the Schnitzers' spiritual sterility are the
plastic flowers and plants in their home and the horde of weedkilling
chemicals that Herman Schnitzer has stored in a shed. Indeed, his
goal is to rid Eden Hills of all weeds, even if it means a complete
sterilization of nature. Ironically enough, the one thing that he does
want to keep alive, a large elm tree that shades his swimming pool, is
dying a slow and ugly death, dropping its dead leaves into the pool.
"The other part of his dream," however, "was realized. No living
thing save humans ever troubled the pool or the tree or the grass"
(53).

But Herman Schnitzer's extermination obsession does not stop
with plant life; he would, if he could, wipe out all Negroes, Jews,
Communists, hillbillies, and anyone else standing in the way of his
version of the American Dream. He refused to help Susie's grandmother clear her name when she was accused of un-American activities; he has furnished his home with a bomb shelter against the attack he is certain will one day come; he insists that his family par-
ticipate in target practice; and he sends Brandon, Susie's younger
brother, to a camp run by what Susie describes as a "super, super
'Save the U.S.A. for Freedom' group . . . . Anybody who admired
Hitler might go for them. Big on preparedness; show the 'dirty communists we mean business,' and all that jazz. Eager for the bomb, for
they'll be generals in heaven when they die" (148).

In short, Herman Schnitzer lives in a world motivated by fear —
fear that his neighborhood will be overrun by weeds and Negroes
and fear that his nation will be overrun by draft resisters, peace
marchers, and subversives. "Hanging's too good for them," he
shouts at a dinner party, "and I include all these old women who
mouth around about peace" (257). This fear, as well as the hate that
it breeds, precludes any true feeling or understanding for Susie or

anyone like her. Susie privately refers to him as "Bismarck" or as her "militant" father. Yet, flabby caricature that he is in the novel, he is also power incarnate; and, though that power is sustained by a dead dream, it is power nonetheless.

Mrs. Schnitzer, actually of Italian descent and once a Catholic, has learned well how to fit into the WASP life her husband has fashioned for them. She has even learned to accept the term "dago" when Herman mouths it in one of his fits of castigation. In the early struggling years of their marriage, she worked in Herman's office; now, however, she is relegated to the background, keeping busy with the supervising of her one fulltime servant, taking beauty treatments, going to club meetings, doing church work, and participating in the many other activities befitting a woman of her station. But to Susie she is more the "Popsicle Queen" — a woman who is really not totally alive — than she is a true mother. She is not so full of hate and fear as Herman; but, like the society around her, she reflects a debilitating artificiality. Susie, in her own mind, describes her mother:

"The woman's hair is an arrangement of lemon popsicles. Her eyes are shavings of blueberry popsicles. Her cheeks are painted plastic lilies in the graveyard six months after the funeral. Her voice is the tinkling of glass from the five-and-ten. Her body is teflon coated.

"She is not always a Popsicle Queen. Mornings very early her face is a frozen pizza, a very old one, so long left unsold the round salami have turned from pink to gray, the cheese is yellow-gray, and the frozen dough is the gray of blue toilet paper, unflushed in the toilet bowl. Other times the face is a frozen pizza dropped from a shopping bag and stepped on in the store by many feet." (154)

The Schnitzers are representative of a world that, despite — or perhaps because of — its great material progress has lost the sense of divine presence. What ideally should be a new Eden is not. Social conscience and ethical responsibility have been blunted by the insatiable desire for material things and by fear; and the democratic ideal, like the trees that stood in the way of housing developments in Eden Hills, has been burned out or uprooted.

Susie, then, can find no common meeting ground with her parents. Verbal exchanges with her father result as often as not in bellowing on his part — scolding her for her hair style, for the folk music she enjoys, for not knowing whether there are any "niggers" in her school. Those with her mother consist "chiefly of questions put in and answers pulled out at a cautious crawl," reminding Susie "of an information desk in some gone-to-sleep airport where you asked into a receiver, and the answer came back to leave you wondering if you had spoken to a human being or a sound track geared to an IBM machine" (136).

Not only is Susie alienated from her parents, she is also alienated from her school. She, along with her friends, sees it merely as one more arm of The Establishment, dedicated not to a genuine search for truth but to keeping itself and Eden Hills "free of Reds and Blacks." As one boy sums it up in responding to a comment that the school paper should not get involved in anything political, "In Eden Hills High that computer curtain hides a million dirty spots; but mention of one in the school paper would show the school was not perfect. There's lots of money here; criticize the school and you go knocking holes in the Free Enterprise System. So, keep all ugly stories where ugliness belongs — among the poor, the Negroes, the goons, and the grease in inner Detroit, or some white suburb of little boxes" (206). Neither is the Vietnam war ever discussed by teachers in the school, nor is it ever mentioned in memorial assemblies. "Nobody," thinks Susie, "could have known from the orations whether the dead students had been killed in the Revolutions or fighting Indians; all had ' — given their lives to bring peace and freedom to the world.' Ugh" (288).

II   *I Am Not My Father*

From her grandmother's people Susie has inherited a sense of the eternal and the transcendental that enables her to hold to the possibility of a world in which basic human relationships can be enjoyed without fear or restriction. She wonders, for example, about the original owner of the old farm house that stands near her own modern home:

Had he ever been back to try and find his cow spring that used to be on what became the Schnitzer front lawn? Did his wife wonder on the daffodil bloom or miss the smell of lilacs in the early morning? Be nice if you could go biking up to that farmhouse and say when someone came to the door: "How do you do. Pardon me, but I'm Susie Schnitzer, your neighbor." Children had used to do that in Highland Park — or was it some other place? Somewhere in the twilights the neighbors had talked across their fence, and exchanged flowers along with smoke from cookout fires. And even in that last place in the northwest corner, the neighbors had spoken now and then. (156)

But she recognizes that such communication is virtually·impossible in Eden Hills and, moreoever, that only when she is away from the prying eyes of the adult world can she be herself. In this context, Susie's love for nature is significant.

Juxtaposed against the excavations for new homes and the burned-off trees and torn-out earth is the pond owned by The Primitive. A refuge from dump trucks, bull-dozers, and huge earth movers standing "like warring monsters ready to charge" (61), the pond is, as it were, the real Eden of Eden Hills — a place of killdeers, red-winged blackbirds, muskrats, frogs, ducks, and a blue heron. To Susie, the pond symbolizes a vital alternative to the dead world around her; and, as such, it affords Susie and her friends a spiritual sustenance and a sense of freedom.

This power of the pond is illustrated when on one visit Susie meets Iggy at the pond. Her first feeling is one of annoyance that her privacy has been invaded; but, as she and Iggy talk, she learns that he too has his own road to walk. At first, Susie is cautious in their conversation, keeping her internal computer in good working order. Soon, however, as they share his thermos of chocolate in a kind of spontaneous communion, they begin sharing past experiences. Some moments later, when they hear music coming from The Primitive's barn, where some of their friends are practicing in a little combo, Iggy grasps Susie's hands, and the two of them dance on a huge rock in an almost ritualistic innocence. After this incident Susie realizes that she can talk to Iggy freely; and the "story of her bedevilment by the student of psychology seemed to pour out as if from some gone-wild tape recorder with no turn-off switch; one that must go on to the end of the tape done in a squeaky, scared-stiff voice that at times seemed sound only" (75-76).

The pond, however, lives on borrowed time; it is threatened by the encroachments of "civilization." While at the pond one day about dusk, Susie sees construction workers firing huge piles of oil-soaked trees, turning the whole area into a nightmare of death and destruction:

The flames, higher, closer, redder, changed the place into a world she had never seen. The barkless patches of trunk left by bulldozer blades on the yet-standing trees became bloody red wounds that with the darkness behind them seemed alive, moving in the leaping light of the flames. A piece of drainpipe crosswise of the road became a black cavernous mouth ringed with red; others, lengthwise, were red-blacked reptilian monsters. The line of earth-destroying machines she had looked at yesterday now appeared as one long red and black beast, wriggling, readying itself to obliterate the earth; for in the wavering bonfire light, red reflections on metal were constantly changing into black shadowy mouths that spread to become black bodies, so that the whole seemed alive and moving.

She looked away to search out a sad, mixed-up chorus, half a quacking, half a terrified crying. She saw soon, low above the trees on the other side of the last bonfire, the wavering, bobbing stream of little shapes. They were ducks, lost and blinded by the fire as they tried to find their summer's nesting grounds, now under the road-fill and fire. They dropped lower to circle aimlessly; a few were able to rise high enough to get away, but most flapped lower and closer above the fire. Soon, they were no longer ducks flying, but only the litter of the world falling into the fire, or, with feathers aflame, whirled away in the updraft. (170)

Mrs. Arnow drew the idea for this fictional pond from a real pond, one on the Arnow property not far from Ann Arbor. When the Arnows first moved there in 1950, the whole area was a place of fruit trees, shrubs, wild flowers, and brush honeysuckle. Their own land was "a reservoir of animal and plant life native to south central Michigan. It was in our woods I learned the beauty of a hawk's flight, and their troubled cries when danger came near; a family nested in a tall, broken topped maple. One morning at first light a buck, doe, and fawn sprang up in the lower lawn and went racing away. Often at dawn I would see a Great Blue Heron flying low above the tree tops on his way to feed in some nearby swamp."[2] But change came to Ann Arbor, just as it did to Eden Hills; and, instead of a place for hiking and biking, the road by the Arnow land became

only something to take you and the car where you had to go. The road was also a place where I went at intervals to pick up the trash, chiefly empty beer bottles and cans, the speeding public threw in front of our fence. The road was now a barren, ugly place, unshaded in the summer's heat, ice choked in winter. Increased traffic had called for a widening; many of the elms had already died; the widening took all the locust, most of the maples and oaks along with other trees on the road shoulders; weed killer had taken not only the flowers but also the wonderful assortment of native shrubs and vines up to and beyond our fence. Two or three years later poison ivy, coarse grass, and a tough variety of goldenrod began to take over the barren spots.[3]

The pond in the novel, interestingly enough, is owned by a woman called The Primitive — really Gertie Nevels of *The Dollmaker,* who has finally found her piece of land. She would have "little hills if I can't have big hills" (306). At the time of the story, she is fighting to keep the builders and weed-sprayers from defiling her land; and she even takes a shot at some of the latter. "Imagine doing all that for weeds," says Herman Schnitzer. "She belongs in an institution" (88). The Primitive and Susie thus have much in common. Indeed, in one sense Susie is Gertie — of a different generation and of a different background, but with the same love of nature and freedom. Having more in common with Gertie than with her parents, the youngster comes to love the Primitive's place:

> Better than mere seeing was the doing. She would never have believed a place inland could have so many interesting jobs — from getting down hay for hungry cattle to washing butter fresh from the churn. And as they talked together, she learned The Primitive's language; she now knew that Bender, the big, friendly black and tan dog, was a cur-dog, not a feist, the look and feel and taste of "strung okrie" and what a diddle was. She learned the glory of walking in the sugar bush late in the afternoon when the long, low rays of the setting sun added yet more gilding to the red and gold leaves over her head and around her feet. (276)

Susie's love of nature, however, goes beyond the calm beauty of the pond; it extends to the sea, with all its vast freedom and elemental power. Like Max in *The Dollmaker,* Susie constantly yearns for the sea — partly because it represents a freedom and power and partly because it recalls happy times at her grandmother's in Nova Scotia. The sea, too powerful for man to destroy, requires no secrets, no protecting of one's integrity through lies and tricks. On the contrary, it demands a total commitment on the part of those who are drawn to it — and, in return, it engenders within them a spiritual as well as a physical vitality. Susie sees her grandmother's people in this light:

> Over and beyond these were the men who made their livings or their starvings by the sea, the fishermen and sailors. Many all mixed up, like a working sea captain her grandmother knew, declaring he hated the North Atlantic, the cruelty of it, the treachery, shaking his fist at it, cursing the day he had wedded it; at last he had taken a "good job" on land with an export company — in less than six months so eager was he for the sea he had shipped as a first mate, unwilling to wait for a captaincy to come up.
>
> Others were like Driving Pete. His young years spent inland as a lumberjack, he had come late to the sea; his sorrows were that all his working life had not been spent at sea, and he was now too old for anything but short-

voyage fishing boats. The sea had taken her great-grandmother's husband and her one son-in-law. Yet she wanted to die within sight and sound of it. (307-08)

A dramatic incident that underlies this feeling that Susie has regarding the sea occurs when she joins a group of her friends on a boat ride on Lake Erie. Robert Kedrick, whose father owns the boat, is not an accomplished sailor and does not heed the gale warnings that are posted. Only by the quick thinking and practical seamanship of Susie and Ben Holmes, a Negro youth, is the boat kept from being capsized. While the sea may symbolize complete freedom, a sailor nevertheless must establish a right relationship with it, or drown. Susie and Ben know this and establish that relationship — just as so many of Mrs. Arnow's characters have done before them — and, when they do, they not only become a "part of the world instead of one more ticketed coffin waiting for burial in a killed and frozen land" (235), but enjoy a sense of exhilaration:

No longer afraid, she gave herself up to an enjoyment of the world. The waves were getting higher, whitecaps curling, breaking into waterfalls, their spray streaming like smoke in the wind. She watched a wave, the biggest yet, roll over the bow, then listened to the crashing, breaking, trickling as it whomped over the wheelhouse. She shivered with the joy of a long hunger, never completely satisfied, but less gnawing now — it was being fed. As they neared Erie, more and more waves smacked the top deck, but the *Antiname* creaked happily on, and the Negro seemed as confident as the boat. (238)

The beauty of the sea, then, is not a beauty concocted out of pretty things to be enjoyed with serenity, but something hard, fine, heroic, and real, wrested out of hardship endured. It is this kind of beauty that Susie sees in the *Antiname,* which at one time, before someone had "modernized" it, had been a working boat. To her, it represents a connection to the past, in much the same way that Gertie's old water bucket does in *The Dollmaker.* Indeed, she cannot "separate the boat and her first owner. Some Nova Scotia fisherman a long time ago on some little bay had, like her grandfather when he was young, worked and saved and dreamed until he could have her built to make his living or his starving by" (226). Susie recognizes that Robert had no affection for the boat. He "worked among those old dead dreams and never wondered on the other owners. He was business all the way" (307), his one thought being to get the boat from here to there. It is Susie who in her own mind christens the boat *Antiname* because for it to have any name other than its now unknown original name would be a kind of desecration. Names moreover, are confining; they belong, therefore, more to the land world of condition than to the sea world of freedom.

II   *Where O Where Is Dear Little Susie?*

At fifteen, Susie is leaving behind the world of childhood and moving into the world of adulthood; and, as Holden Caulfield in Salinger's *The Catcher in the Rye* learns, the transition is not easy. She yearns for a sense of security, yet she does not want overprotectiveness. She recalls how her Uncle Lans had rescued her when she was six years old from a group of children who were beating her and shoving mud in her mouth because of her grandmother's supposedly un-American activities; how the kind Dr. Laughton has always been concerned about her health, both physical and mental; and more recently how The Primitive had watched over her while she roamed the pond and the land. On the other hand, she understands her friend Iggy when he says that overprotectiveness "is just another name for nosiness, or the quieting of guilt feelings brought on by rejection of the child" (74).

Susie is in some respects a female counterpart to Holden Caulfield of *The Catcher in the Rye*. Both are aware of the hypocrisy and apparent lack of compassion that mark the adult world, and both have a romantic attraction to the past as a representation of something fixed — an order that contrasts with the anxiety and chaos of the contemporary world. Holden looks to the museum and to his dead brother Allie; Susie, to her early life with her grandmother and to such things as the *Antiname* when it belonged to its original owner. Holden, vacillating between the child world and adult world, has a pervasive fear of disappearing. Susie has something of the same feeling when Robert, instead of taking her out to dinner, leaves her to study alone in the public library while he keeps a rendezvous with an older woman:

She stood alone still and watched the car crawl back into the line of traffic. All the jewels were gone from the lights. The friendly rain was only soot-blackened water, cold on your ankles, and colder as it caught you on the back of the neck. She turned away, and as in childhood lifted her face to search out the stone faces that ringed the library. She stared, searching, rain falling on her face, until from two steps higher a voice asked, that of a man, well bred to understand that one should not frighten girls by coming too close: "May I help you, little girl?"

"The faces," she answered, not turning her head, "I can't find them."

"They are still there," he said, a hint of anger in his voice, "but washed so clean by some modern method, you can scarcely see them or read their names. They haven't changed places; they're still on the Woodward side. It's the library that's changed. Now, most people enter as you are, from Cass."

She said: "Oh. — I forgot. — I've been here many times — since — since they washed the faces." She tried to see the man's face, but could not as he was two steps above her, and now holding the umbrella over her. "Thank you," she said, and went on up the steps.

The umbrella stayed above her until she reached an outer glass door, and the man said: "Remember — always — the faces are still there."

"I won't forget again," she said. (317-18) The library then is to Susie what the museum is to Holden.

Both Susie and Holden are idealistic in their life goals. Holden's is the symbolic goal of becoming a catcher in the rye, of catching children in their innocence before they fall over the cliff of experience. Susie's is "to be a doctor, and work with children; try — well, not just to cure their bodies, but hope to help them into happiness — if possible" (212). Both know how difficult happiness is to achieve. And perhaps that knowledge explains why Holden keeps his goal a symbolic one, one that he can't ever realize, and why Susie qualifies hers with the words "hope" and "if possible."

In the end, Susie, of course, is the stronger of the two characters. Holden is unable to throw anything against the world but a red hunting cap that he wears backwards. Susie, on the other hand, beats the world at its own game. At the end of *The Catcher in the Rye,* Holden is left with the feeling of missing people — an indication, to be sure, that he is on the way to a reconciliation of his ideals with the realities of society. At the end of *The Weedkiller's Daughter,* however, Susie knows that she has won. When she leaves the interview with the psychologist, she does so with a feeling of triumph and personal freedom:

She'd lived through the pain; and this time she would know exactly what she had said. In those other sessions with the man last year she'd put the little tape recorder in her binder, but afraid to leave it on her desk, she had held it on her knees; reception had been so poor she never knew — .

Oh, yes, she did know now. She knew he hadn't learned any of her secrets. He hadn't learned.

She paused a moment at the head of the stairs. She'd had the feeling she was supposed to meet somebody or do something. She rushed on; it didn't matter; anything important she would have remembered. In spite of the pain it was good to move again and know that Susan Schnitzer still belonged to Susan Schnitzer. (372)

Artistically speaking, *The Weedkiller's Daughter* does not reach the level of quality of Mrs. Arnow's previous works. There is an air of the contrived about it. Incidents and characters, instead of growing out of the story, seem to have been set in like so many building blocks — with the result that they do not seem real. Even Susie is not always a believable character; indeed, like her teenage friends, she is often trite and too good. Moreover, the powerful scenes so often evoked in *Hunter's Horn* and *The Dollmaker* are missing in this book.

Yet, even with the above limitations, *The Weedkiller's Daughter* does not entirely fail; for it touches in no small way on the generation gap of its time. It speaks for the generation of young of the 1960's — disillusioned yet idealistic, naive yet wise beyond their years; and to understand Susie Schnitzer is, in a sense, to understand that generation — a generation that grew up with the specter of the H-bomb and the visible horror and apparent meaninglessness of the Vietnam war, only to find itself on the threshold of another terrifying situation — a world threatened with ecological destruction. Young people, of course, have always rebelled in some way against the authority of the adult world, but in the end they have for the most part been assimilated into and become part of that world. For every outcast Huck Finn, there have been a hundred conventional Tom Sawyer's. In the end, perhaps, Susie Schnitzer's generation will follow the same pattern; but the very fact that so many recent American fiction writers have turned to the adolescent as a metaphor indicates a belief that youth, if not in a practical at least in an abstract sense, can provide a dream for a society that seems desperately in need of one. Therein lies the importance of *The Weedkiller's Daughter.*

CHAPTER 8

Artistic Vision

T HAT Harriette Arnow will go down in the American literary chronicle as a major figure is, at this point at least, highly improbable. Four conventionally written novels — in a time, unfortunately, when such have not been readily accepted by critics and scholars as being on the cutting edge of creativity — are hardly enough to establish her in the major category. As an artist, however, she certainly needs no defense. A Realist who rejects such things as experimental forms, complex plots, sentimental themes, the pyrotechnics of sex, and the contemporary mania for neurotic protagonists, she combines in her work a penetrating and sensitive insight into the human condition with a lean prose style — a combination that has been responsible for a literary output that, though thin in quantity, is abundant in quality.

Reflecting on modern stylistic trends in literature in a paper presented at the Book and Author Luncheon of the Special Libraries Association Convention in Detroit in 1955, Mrs. Arnow decried what she regarded as a movement away from simplicity in writing to complexity:

But today our modern literature, the work of most of the big five, productions labeled as art, reflect something of the feeling of the age that mankind is not worth the study of the artist; that art and its medium belong to a world which too often only the initiated can enter. Once men attempted to convey complex thoughts in simple words and though sentences might be long they were based on a long study of the language. Today we often cannot find the thought for the complexity of words. A sentence can be loaded down with useless whiches, average five prepositions to every verb, violate all rules of grammar, and wander thus for two pages. Still, if it be comprehensible to the learned few it is art; the fewer who can understand, the greater the art is held to be. Thus our young ones who would write poetry and novels look not to the world for inspiration, nor to a period of apprenticeship to learn a craft; craftsmanship is out, and art springs forth full-blown. There are learned ones to criticize and explain; only the few can understand the criticism. Literature is not for the masses but for the student of literature, and unlike former times, people learned in other fields but uninitiated in modern literary symbolism cannot enter. They can follow the literary artist no more than the literary artist can understand a paper concerned with some chemical change brought about by a nitrogen-fixing bacterial. I often think, in all this hue and cry over atomic secrets, that if only scientists could invent a language as obscure as much of that of our modern literary art, we need never worry again over atomic leaks.[1]

Some years later, in another discussion of style in writing, she stated, "I think a mistake the young make is studying style over-much — say of such a writer as Faulkner. Style alone does not make a writer, and I'm happy to say that I think there is less emphasis on style now than there was a few years ago. I prefer reading the letters and journals of such a one as Stendahl, who wanted no style, who wanted his writing to be as clear and concise as a police report."[2]

A reader of any of Mrs. Arnow's works would surely agree that her writing is clear and concise — not so much, perhaps, as a police report, but certainly enough so that her story-lines, her characters, and her descriptions are not obstructed by verbal effusion or highly stylized rhetoric. Using short, precise strokes, she evokes a mood, paints a scene, focuses on a dramatic moment, or isolates some aspect of a character that makes him live for the reader. The result is a style that serves as an unobtrusive and artistically effective vehicle for Mrs. Arnow's themes.

In her writing, then, Mrs. Arnow has been content to be a simple storyteller, attempting to record honestly the nature of human experience as she conceives it. Her mountain fiction, for example, goes beyond the mere local-color approach that marked that genre for so long. More than just presenting the sights, sounds, beliefs, customs, institutions, and such of the area and its people, she brings out the tragedies and ironies engendered in a severely isolated and circumscribed way of life. In the same way, she casts a hard light on the environmental and social conditions that limit her characters in urban settings — a housing project in *The Dollmaker* and an exclusive suburb in *The Weedkiller's Daughter*.

Background, of course, is of great significance in this process. In reminiscing about her own reading choices, Mrs. Arnow remarked, "I know there are novels and novels, but I have always enjoyed reading a novel with background that takes me sometimes into an entirely different world. When I was in my early teens, I first read Thomas Hardy; and I could feel a kinship, because his characters were in hills and woods — different from what I knew; but the backgrounds merged with the people."[3] In this comment, she might well have been talking about her own work. Sense of place, for example, could hardly be more strongly evoked than it is in *Hunter's Horn* and *The Dollmaker;* and the same could be said to a somewhat lesser degree of *Mountain Path.* Only in *The Weedkiller's Daughter* does this sense seem diminished — the reason perhaps being that Mrs. Arnow was writing not so much from experience as from observation, and thus she was a little less sure of her material.

Through all of Mrs. Arnow's fiction, character rather than plot shapes the stories. In discussing how *Hunter's Horn* came about, for example, she explained that it started with a man.[4] She had never owned a fox hound, but she had heard of men obsessed with fox hunting — forever hunting but very seldom getting; for a good, swift, young fox is elusive indeed. Out of it all came Nunn Ballew, a man who drops everything to hunt a fox — a man whom Mrs. Arnow does not see as worthless and irresponsible, but as one whom she "rather loved."[5] He was, she said, "no different from the modern businessman who sacrifices all for position and money in the business world."[6] These views of Nunn are interesting because they underscore what the reader sees reflected in the stories. First, Mrs. Arnow is able to instill individuality in types. Second, she is able to project herself into her characters — seeing things the way they see them. Third, she does not evaluate her characters, either ethically or morally — letting their actions speak for themselves. Fourth, she gives her characters a universal significance.

Of Mrs. Arnow's characters, the women stand out as the strongest and the most fully developed. Other than Nunn in *Hunter's Horn,* no male character is developed to any real degree. The reason for this lack of significant male characters is not that Mrs. Arnow is unable to portray men, because as her treatment of Nunn illustrates, she can project herself into the male psyche as well as into the female one. Perhaps it is engendered in her feeling that American literature has exhibited a paucity of truly substantial women characters.[7] In an interview with Evelyn Stewart of the *Detroit Free Press* in 1958, she remarked that she hated to "emerge from the Eighteenth Century" because "life was better for women way back then."[8] Though women did not have to compete with men then, they had, in Mrs.

Arnow's mind, more power than now. "And the men didn't hate women then, the way they do now," she went on. "Men and women were yoke-mates, pulling together. Now they're pulling different ways, each trying to manipulate the other and run the other's life."[9] No better example of this view, perhaps, can be found in her own fiction than in the conflict between Gertie and Clovis Nevels in *The Dollmaker.*

Mrs. Arnow's characters, more often than not, are trapped by social restrictions and environmental forces from which they cannot escape. In *Mountain Path,* Chris Bledsoe seeks violence and revenge because they are part of the code under which he has grown up. Louisa knows the potential that is within Chris, but she also knows that it can never be realized in Cal Valley. Time for him has run out, and all that remains is for Louisa to build her future in light of what she has learned.

In *Hunter's Horn,* Milly, Nunn, and Suse — all three — are limited by conditions which they do not fully comprehend. Milly stoically accepts her lot with a fatalistic "Oh, God, it's hard to be a woman."[10] Nunn and Suse both try to escape: Nunn, through chasing King Devil; Suse, through dreaming of a life in the outside world. When Nunn's chase is finished, he, too, is in a sense finished. By condemning Suse, he has reverted to a viewpoint common enough among his neighbors, but which he for a time had escaped. Suse has never tasted the pleasures nor felt the opportunities of the outside world, but she knows that somewhere there exists a place better than Little Smokey Creek — a place where excitement abounds and where love is possible. She doesn't really learn from Lureenie's experiences that the outside world also has its relentless forces that can grind one to the ground.

In *The Dollmaker,* Gertie Nevels learns firsthand of such forces in the world away from the mountains. She sees her family come apart: Reuben rejects Detroit and returns home; Clytie and Enoch drift away from the old traditions amid the pressures to conform; and Cassie is killed because she is unable to express her own innocent version of love and affection in a world that will not understand. More than learning about city life, Gertie experiences a kind of revelation. Her creative spirit that flourished so freely in Kentucky is crushed in Detroit, but in return she achieves an understanding of humanity that was not available to her before. Whether the price she pays is too great is left for the reader to decide.

In *The Weedkiller's Daughter,* Susie Schnitzer serves as a contemporary illustration of the theme of the individual versus the human condition. She is Louisa Sheridan, Suse Ballew, Gertie Nevels embodied in a teenaged girl. Wise beyond her years and clever almost beyond belief, Susie rejects everything that militates against her being herself. She triumphs — at least temporarily. In doing so, she is not so much a real person as she is a symbol of what Mrs. Arnow has been driving at all along — that only when one searches out and nourishes his own natural yearnings and only when he learns humility and compassion can he truly be an individual.

All of Mrs. Arnow's fiction reflects an ironic approach. While she may be simply a storyteller, she does not oversimplify; for life is not to be explained in simple terms or easy philosophies. She knows, and her characters learn, that life is full of contradictions as well as harmonies and that good and evil are not always clearly discernible, but often overlap or fuse. Moreover, while she does not have an uncritical faith in human nature, she does not take a stance of superiority over her characters. She sees them as human beings — often cruel, often kind, and often bewildered by the world in which they live. Nor is she the obvious iconoclast or preacher with regard to human institutions and beliefs. She may, for example, draw devastating pictures of fundamental religion, be it of the Kentucky Protestant variety or of the Detroit Catholic variety, and of the right-wing bigotry of such people as Susie Schnitzer's father; but she does not let thesis impinge upon art. Rather, her characters and their actions speak for themselves — and often eloquently.

Closely related to Mrs. Arnow's ironic point of view is her treatment of nature. Throughout her stories runs the idea that nature, timeless and bigger than man, is the ultimate reality; but it, too, has its ironies. While in all the novels Mrs. Arnow sees an affinity between natural life and moral life, she does not flinch from the threatening aspects of nature. Indeed, the relationship between man and nature is not a reciprocal one so much as it is a one-sided one. It is man that must adapt to nature, for only in a correct adaptation can he find real sustenance; and this lesson is what many of Mrs. Arnow's characters either know or learn. Nunn Ballew, for example, discovers the folly of making nature (the fox in his case) a symbol of something more than it is. King Devil is neither good nor evil but merely a fox trying to stay alive in the world in much the same way that Nunn is. Nunn, by attributing malice to the fox, suffers from an intellectual and moral misconception of the way things are. He does not understand what Susie Schnitzer does — that man's dignity comes not from a foolhardy defiance of nature but from a recognition and acceptance of its beauty and power. And the same may be said for a recognition and acceptance of a man's worth — what Gertie Nevels learns.

Thus, while most of Mrs. Arnow's stories could not be said to have unqualified happy endings, they do not hum the umbra's note to the extent that the works of so many contemporary American authors do. She is not, to be sure, a rear-guard romanticist, but neither is she one who has lost hope in the present and future of man. She recognizes that human plans do not always coincide with the way things go. She also recognizes, however, that man has within him a certain indomitable spirit that, though occasionally stifled, can never be permanently erased. Nitro Joe in "Marigolds and Mules," for example, may be blown to bits in an ugly oil field, but the genuine love he had for pretty flowers is no less real. And the world may defeat Suse Ballew, but her counterpart, Susie Schnitzer, at least for the moment, prevails.

Writing for Mrs. Arnow, as she put it, "has been very hard work. But people don't realize it. I recall an editor who said about one of my two later fiction books, 'The ending just wrote itself, didn't it?' Very little of my writing — sometimes there's been a good streak when it goes forward — has written itself. Most of it has been very difficult work after a good deal of thought."[11] The duties of wife and mother have no doubt impinged upon her writing career. Yet, in another sense, those duties, along with the wild flowers she still nurtures, reflect the very "going-on" of life that so predominantly marks all of her writing, be it fiction or history. Both her life and her literary contribution offer proof that the worthwhile is often attainable only through the proper application; conversely, the "labor of the file" increases the depth and significance of the act of living and heightens the sensitivity and charm of the resultant literary expression. One offers thanks to Mrs. Simpson for that second-hand typewriter and to Harriette Simpson Arnow for her resistance to knitting needles.

Notes and References

Preface

1. From a taped reminiscence by Mrs. Arnow. Hereafter referred to as Tape.

2. John Bradbury, *Renaissance in the South* (Chapel Hill, 1963), P. 5.

3. *Ibid.*

4. Louis Rubin, "The Difficulties of Being a Southern Writer Today: Or, Getting Out from Under William Faulkner," *The Journal of Southern History, XXIX (Nov. 1963), 486-94.*

Chapter One

1. Peter Schrag, "Appalachia: Again the Forgotten Land," *Saturday Review,* Jan. 27, 1968, P. 14.

2. *Seedtime on the Cumberland* (New York, 1960), P. 4.

3. *Ibid.,* P. 39.

4. *Ibid.,* P. 39.

5. Tape.

6. From an unpublished manuscript in the University of Kentucky Library entitled "On Being Asked to Write a Dog Story."

7. *Ibid.*

8. *Ibid.*

9. *Ibid.*

10. *Ibid.*

11. *Ibid.*

12. *Seedtime,* p. 16.

13. From unpublished notes of Harriette Arnow in the University of Kentucky Library.

14. *Ibid.*

15. *Ibid.*

16. Tape.

17. Copy of a letter from Harriette Arnow to Harold Strauss, 1939. In University of Kentucky Library.

18. Tape.

19. Tape.

20. Tape.

21. Tape.

22. Copy of a letter from Harriette Arnow to Harold Strauss, undated. In University of Kentucky Library.

23. Tape.

24. Letter from Harold Strauss to Harriette Arnow, March 12, 1936. In University of Kentucky Library.

25. *Ibid.*

26. *Ibid.*

27. Tape.

28. Copy of a letter from Harriette Arnow to Harold Strauss, undated. In University of Kentucky Library.

29. Tape.

30. Tape.

31. Tape.

32. Tape.

Chapter Two

1. Harriette Simpson, *Mountain Path* (New York, 1936), p. 8. Subsequent page references to this book in Chapter 2 will appear in parentheses following the quotation.

Chapter Three

1. Harriette Simpson, "Marigolds and Mules," *Kosmos,* III (Aug.-Sept., 1934), 3-6.

2. Harriette Simpson, "A Mess of Pork," *The New Talent,* I (Oct.-Dec. 1935), 4-11.

3. Harriette Simpson, "Washerwoman's Day," *Southern Review,* I, 3 (1936), 522-27.

4. Harriette Simpson, "The Hunter," *Atlantic,* CLXXIV (Nov., 1944), 79-84.

Chapter Four

1. *Hunter's Horn* (New York, 1949), p. 56. Subsequent to this book in Chapter 4 appear in parentheses following the quotation.

2. Anonymous Letter to Harriette Arnow, Undated.

3. Herschel Brickell, Review of *Hunter's Horn, New York Times,* May 29, 1949, p. 4.

Chapter Five

1. *The Dollmaker* (New York, 1954), p. 571. Subsequent page references to this book in Chapter 5 appear in parentheses following the quotation.

Chapter Six

1. *Seedtime on the Cumberland* (New York, 1960), p. vii. Subsequent page references to this book in Chapter 6 appear in parentheses following the quotation.

2. Donald Davidson, Review of *Seedtime on the Cumberland,* New York *Herald Tribune Book Review,* Sept. 4, 1960, p. 1.

3. *Flowering of the Cumberland* (New York, 1963), pp. v-vi. Subsequent page references to this book in Chapter 6 appear in parentheses following the quotation.

Chapter Seven

1. *The Weedkiller's Daughter* (New York, 1970), p. 45. Subsequent page references to this book in Chapter 7 will appear in parentheses following the quotation.

2. "Some Musings on the Nature of History," *The Clarence M. Burton Memorial Lecture* (Historical Society of Michigan), p. 6.

3. *Ibid.,* p. 8.

Chapter Eight

1. Harriette Arnow, "Language — The Key That Unlocks All the Boxes," *Wilson Library Bulletin,* XXX (May, 1956). 685.

2. Tape.

3. Tape.

4. Tape.

5. Tape.

6. Tape.

7. Tape.

8. Interview, *Detroit Free Press,* April 6, 1958.

9. *Ibid.*

10. *Hunter's Horn,* p. 68.

11. Tape.

Selected Bibliography

PRIMARY SOURCES

1. Novels

The Dollmaker. New York: Macmillan, 1954. Reprinted in 1961 and 1965 by Collier Books.

Hunter's Horn. New York: Macmillan, 1949.

Mountain Path. New York: Covici Friede, 1936. Reprinted in 1963 by The Council of the Southern Mountains.

The Weedkiller's Daughter. New York: Alfred Knopf, 1970.

2. Social Histories

Flowering of the Cumberland. New York: Macmillan, 1963.

Seedtime on the Cumberland. New York: Macmillan, 1960.

3. Short Stories

"The Hunter." *Atlantic,* CLXXIV (Nov., 1944), 79-84.

"Marigolds and Mules." *Kosmos,* III (Aug.-Sept., 1934), 3-6.

"A Mess of Pork." *The New Talent,* I (Oct.-Dec., 1935), 4-11.

"Washerwoman's Day." *Southern Review,* I, 3 (1936), 522-27.

4. Essays

"Language — The Key That Unlocks All the Boxes." *Wilson Library Bulletin,* XXX (May, 1956), 683-85.

"The Gray Woman of Appalachia." *Nation,* CCXI (December 28, 1970), 684-87.

"Progress Reached Our Valley." *Nation,* CCXI (August 3, 1970), 71-77.

"Some Musings on the Nature of History." The Clarence M. Burton Memorial Lecture, delivered on October 18, 1968, at the Michigan Museums Conference in Kalamazoo, Michigan. Reprinted in pamphlet form.

"Voices over the Mountains." *Mountain Life and Work: The Magazine of the Appalachian South,* XLI (Spring, 1965), 4.

5. Manuscripts and Letters

The University of Kentucky Library has numerous manuscripts (some unpublished) and letters to and from Mrs. Arnow.

SECONDARY SOURCES

To date there have been no significant studies dealing with the works of Harriette Arnow.

Index

Ahab, Captain, 72, 73
Anderson, Mrs. *(The Dollmaker)*, 99
Andrew, Old *(Hunter's Horn)*, 82
Angus *(The Weedkiller's Daughter)*, 111
Antiname (The Weedkiller's Daughter), 118-19
Appalachia, 17
Arnow, Harold, 40-42, 43
Arnow, Harriette: character, 124-25; childhood games, 21-22; childhood stories, 22-23, 101; early reading, 23-25; early writing, 25, 28, 30-31, 38-39; education, 25, 28, 29-30, 31-33, 35-36, 46; family, 18, 21, 22, 23, 25, 26-27, 28, 31, 35, 40-42, 43, 44, 127; irony, 126-27; marriage, 40-42; realism, 40, 45, 64-65; style, 54-55, 56, 83-84, 100, 107-109, 116, 121, 122-23, 124-27; first teaching position, 33-35
Arnow, Marcella, 41, 42
Arnow, Thomas, 42
Atlantic Monthly, 41, 61
Attakullakulla (Cherokee half-chief), 104

Ballew family *(Hunter's Horn)*, 63
Ballew, Milly *(Hunter's Horn)*, 64, 65, 67, 68, 69, 74-77, 80, 82-83, 125
Ballew, Nunnelly *(Hunter's Horn)*, 42, 61-62, 63-64, 66-67, 69-74, 75, 76, 77, 78, 80-81, 82, 83, 110, 111, 124, 125, 126-27
Ballew, Suse *(Hunter's Horn)*, 44, 64, 68, 69, 74, 77, 78-83, 110, 111, 125, 126, 127
Barnetts *(Mountain Path)*, 48-49, 53
Battle John Brand *(Hunter's Horn)*, 68-69, 72-73, 79, 88-89, 95, 97
Berea College, 31-33

Between the Flowers, 39, 40
Bible, 24, 28, 31, 68, 72, 74, 79, 80, 81, 88, 89, 90-91, 98
Bingham, George C., 17
Blare *(Hunter's Horn)*, 67
Bledsoe, Chris *(Mountain Path)*, 45, 48, 49, 50, 51, 52-53, 125
Bolin, Clarie ("Washerwoman's Day"), 60, 61
Bolin, Laurie Mae ("Washerwoman's Day"), 60, 61
Book and Author Luncheon of the Special Libraries Association Convention, Detroit, 1955, 122-23
Boone, Daniel, 17
Brickell, Herschel, 84
Buchanan, John *(Flowering of the Cumberland)*, 105, 106
Buchanan, Sally *(Flowering of the Cumberland)*, 105, 106
Bunyan, John, 24
Burnside High School, 28, 29-30
Burnside, Kentucky, 18-19, 21, 23, 26, 28, 30, 33, 34, 38, 101

Calhoun, Corie *(Mountain Path)*, 47-48, 49, 50, 51, 52, 75
Calhoun, Lee Buck *(Mountain Path)*, 46, 47, 48-49, 50, 51, 52, 53
Calhoun, Rie *(Mountain Path)*, 47, 49, 50, 51, 52, 78
Calhoun (Cal) family, 45-54, 125
Cal Valley, 45, 49, 50-54
Callie Lou *(The Dollmaker)*, 92, 98, 100
Catcher in the Rye, The, 119-20
Caulfield, Holden, 119-20
Chartier, Martin *(Seedtime on the Cumberland)*, 104
Chickamauga, 106